C000061461

E.L. Mascall
1984

114

Christian Theism

CHRISTIAN THEISM
A Study in its Basic Principles

by

HUW PARRI OWEN
Emeritus Professor of Christian Doctrine
King's College, University of London.

T. & T. CLARK
36 GEORGE STREET, EDINBURGH

Copyright © T. & T. Clark, 1984

PRINTED BY
BILLING AND SONS LIMITED, WORCESTER
FOR

T. & T. CLARK, EDINBURGH

ISBN: 0 56709336 0

Preface

The scope of this book is indicated by the title and chapter headings. I have attempted to state as concisely as possible what I consider to be the basic Christian beliefs concerning God and his relation to the world. I write at a time of theological unrest and uncertainty. My own conviction, that will become apparent in the ensuing pages, is that although the lack of any clear divine revelation and the limitations of the human mind compel us to be agnostic on many matters, the main Christian doctrines survive the most rigorous scrutiny. I am convinced that the theological substance of Christian tradition is no less rationally acceptable today than it was in previous ages. The substance, I maintain, is this. God, who exists in the threefold form of Father, Son and Holy Spirit, and who created us out of nothing, so loved us that he became man for us in Christ in order than we, by our free consent, might share in the eternal life that Christ won for us by his victory over evil on the Cross. Interpretations of this substance differ; but the substance itself will always remain; and it differentiates Christianity from all other religions.

I have attempted to give due weight to all the main aspects of Christian theism and not merely to those that happen to evoke immediate interest or controversy. Nevertheless, I hope that this book will constitute my own answers to questions that are prominent in theological discussion today. So far at least as the British scene is concerned, two main questions (that are closely interconnected) have emerged. And these, so far from being minor or of merely passing significance, go to the heart of Christianity. The first (brought to a head by the publication of the symposium entitled *The Myth of God Incarnate*) concerns the status and nature of belief in the Incarnation. The second concerns the relation between Christianity and the truth claims made by non-Christian religions. The first of these questions has always been the major one for Christian theologians. This is inevitable; for Christianity, considered merely as an historical phenomenon, is indissolubly bound, in some way, to belief in Christ as the mediator of salvation. The second question, though not wholly new, obviously gains a new significance from the growing interest (caused by various factors) in non-Christian religions. I have discussed both questions in this book. And I have devoted a whole chapter to the first. But I shall recur to them in an Appendix where I shall examine the answers given to them by John Hick; for I believe that such an examination will illumine them as sharply as possible.

In writing this book I have constantly borne in mind my fellow theologians and university students of theology. However, I hope that the book will also be helpful to all those who have an intellectual interest in Christianity. With this wider range of readers in view I have explained technical terms whenever such an explanation seemed desirable. I have sought to avoid a tedious amount of documentation (although at all essential points I have dealt with views that differ from my own). I have also tried, even when I have been compelled to disagree with other writers, to avoid the polemical and negative tone by which theological writings can so easily be marred. And of course I do not claim any personal infallibility for my views. All that any one theologian can claim is to state the truth as he sees it in the light of his own spiritual response to, and reflection on, the religious tradition he has inherited.

Finally I wish to thank my publishers for suggesting valuable additions to my manuscript.

Huw Owen,
London, 1983

Contents

INTRODUCTION

'Theism' is derived from the Greek *theos,* that means 'God' or 'a god'. As such it tells us nothing; for belief in God or the gods can take a bewildering variety of forms. However, theism has come to stand for belief in one God who totally transcends the world that he made and who is perfect in wisdom, power and love. This is only a minimal definition that I shall expand in chapter one. Yet it is sufficient to distinguish theism from other concepts of God and especially from its two chief rivals: polytheism and pantheism. By affirming that God is one theism excludes polytheism (the view that there are many gods): and by affirming that God totally transcends the world it excludes pantheism (the view that the world is itself divine because it is the self-expression of God's being).

Theism (as I have defined it) has been and still is accepted by Jews, Christians, Muslims and many others who stand outside the Judaeo-Christian tradition. The distinctive contribution of Christianity is threefold. First, Christians believe that God is, not merely one, but also three in one - that he exists in the threefold form of Father, Son and Holy Spirit. Secondly, they believe that the Son became man in Christ. Thirdly, they believe that Christ is the sole means of their salvation. These beliefs are elucidated by the doctrines of the Trinity, the Incarnation and the Atonement. The Christian form of theism is related to non-Christian forms in the following ways.

1. The Christian doctrines I have just stated are wholly new. They cannot be deduced from the theistic beliefs that Christians share with Jews, Muslims and others. They cannot be reached by pure reason. They arose solely from God's revelation of himself in one figure of history - Jesus of Nazareth.

2. This revelation is supernatural. Of course all forms of God's self-revelation are supernatural in the sense that God himself is supernatural. But the Christian form is supernatural in the further and distinctive sense that it is constituted by Christ as God incarnate. Whereas other forms of revelation occur through media that are wholly created, the Christian form occurs in a person who is both human and divine.

3. Nevertheless, Christian revelation presupposes those beliefs that all theists have in common. This is true both historically and logically. It is true historically in so far as the first Christians took for granted the theistic beliefs that had become established in Judaism. It is true logically in so far as these beliefs shaped the development of every

Christian doctrine.

4. Christianity fulfils the fundamental tenets of theism. This again is true both historically and logically. It is true historically in so far as the early Church's understanding of Christ was continuously shaped by the conviction that he fulfilled those beliefs concerning God that were held by both Jews and Greeks. It is true logically in so far as every Christian doctrine can be represented as fulfilling belief in a God who is the Creator of the universe.

Because of 3 and 4, Christian revelation, while being wholly new and supernatural, is still a form of theism. We can, and for certain purposes must, distinguish between the general form of theism that Christians share with non-Christians and the distinctively Christian form that was evolved in the light of Christian revelation. Yet we cannot divorce this revelation from general theism; for the former both presupposes and perfects the latter. In so far as Christian revelation presupposes general theism it is an instance of theism; but in so far as it perfects general theism it is theism *par excellence.* In maintaining this I do no more than apply the maxims that 'grace presupposes nature' and that 'grace perfects nature, not destroys it'.

Unfortunately general theism and Christian revelation are often kept apart. The former is then assigned to the province of the philosophy of religion (or philosophical theology) while the latter is assigned to the province of Christian doctrine (or dogmatic theology). For some purposes this separation is inevitable. Yet for the reasons I gave it cannot be final. From a Christian standpoint a full understanding of God must include both those beliefs that all theists have in common and those that arise only from our response to God's revelation in Christ. The Christian thinker must also show how these beliefs influence each other.

In the succeeding pages I have tried to exhibit the interrelation of general and specifically Christian theism without obscuring the differences between them. Because I believe so strongly in their interrelation I have interwoven them in the order of the topics I have chosen. I do not claim that this order is the only one; but the grounds for my choice are these. I have begun with the concept of creation for the following reasons. The concept signifies the basic form of God's relation to the world; it entails belief in many of the properties that theists ascribe to God; and it shaped the whole christology of the early Church. I deal next with the doctrines of the Incarnation and the Trinity because these add a distinctively Christian dimension to the basic theism implied by the concept of creation. I treat the doctrine of the Incarnation before the doctrine of the Trinity because while the Trinity is prior to the Incarnation in the order of being the doctrine of the Incarnation is prior to the doctrine of the Trinity in the order of knowing. My reasons for discussing next providence and evil are that they arise from belief in God as the Creator and that, from a Christian standpoint, they cannot be adequately assessed apart from the doctrine of the Incarnation. I have withheld discussion of the Atonement until the following chapter because the doctrine of the Atonement implies both the doctrine of the Incarnation and a discussion of evil.

I must state two things concerning the scope and limits of the book. First, because I have chosen to write on the *basic* principles of Christian theism there are some Christian doctrines (chiefly those of the Church and the sacraments) that I shall not examine. Although these doctrines are essential to Christianity they are secondary in the sense that they presuppose, and largely derive their meaning from, the doctrines with which I shall deal. Secondly, this book is devoted entirely to the content of Christian faith, and not at all to the act of faith. I have examined the act of faith, and religious epistemology as a whole, in another book.[1] I still adhere to the views I put forward there. The substance of the matter, I maintain, is as follows.

Faith includes three elements: assent (*assensus*), trust (*fiducia*) and knowledge (*notitia*). We cannot believe in God unless we assent to some propositions concerning him. Also our assent is defective unless it is accompanied by trust in him. Yet our assent and trust would be groundless without knowledge. Faith's knowledge consists in an experience of God as our Creator and Redeemer. This experience has three main characteristics. It is, though direct, always mediated by finite 'signs' of God's presence; it is not due to a separate religious 'faculty', but is a special example of a capacity for intuitive apprehension that we all exercise in our secular existence; and it is obtainable by all human persons because all are made in God's image. Faith is supra-rational in the sense that it is impossible to prove, from premises acceptable to believers and unbelievers equally, that God exists or that he has supernaturally revealed himself. Yet faith is rational in so far as the experience on which it rests is a conformity of the mind to the intelligible structure of divine Being. Hence the propositions it yields must satisfy those rational criteria that are appropriate to it. They must be self-consistent, congruous with the data of secular experience, and (where this is relevant) based on historical evidence. I have tried to meet the demands of these criteria in this book.

There is, however, one further point of religious epistemology that, I now realize, I did not sufficiently stress in my previous book, largely because I was then writing from a philosophical rather than a theological standpoint. This is that specifically Christian (as against generally theistic) faith is a supernatural act in so far as it is inspired by the Holy Spirit who proceeds from Christ, and who enables us to perceive his deity. This perception in turn forms the cognitive basis of the supernatural life that Christ communicates. The totality of Christian revelation is constituted by the Father's self-disclosure *in* the Son and *through* the Holy Spirit. Of course God's action in the world always takes this triune form. In particular the Holy Spirit is always present in the human soul as the source of spiritual and moral truth.

Yet he is supernaturally present in Christians in so far as his function among them is to testify to the Father's supernatural revelation in the incarnate Son. At the same time Christian faith (as I shall maintain in writing on 'grace') occurs through the same natural faculties by which God's sheer existence is apprehended: and its truth claims also are subject to the rational criteria that are appropriate to them.[2]

I have not written this book from the standpoint of any one school of philosophical or theological thought although I have done my best to learn from all schools. All I claim is to state the truth as I see it in the light of my total understanding of scripture and tradition. On the relation between the latter my view is this. Tradition is primary in so far as it signifies everything that has been 'handed on' concerning God's revelation in Christ from the earliest days of the Church until now. It thus includes, not only conciliar pronouncements and the writings of individual theologians, but also the worship of the Church and the experiential testimony of its members. Yet within this continuing tradition the books of the New Testament occupy a uniquely authoritative place if only because they are the earliest record of Christian revelation and were granted canonical status by the early Church. Hence I shall indicate the New Testament's evidence for the doctrines I shall discuss; but of course I must leave a full discussion of it to scholars in this field.

However, although I do not claim to represent any particular type of theology in contrast with other types I inevitably start with a few dominant convictions. I shall state three that have already become apparent and that will emerge continually in the following pages. In stating them I shall indicate my attitude to some of the main strands in twentieth century theology.

1. Theism, and so a knowledge of the God whom Christians worship, exists apart from Christian revelation. This knowledge is not merely conceptual; it can also be experiential; it can mediate communion with God and contribute to a person's salvation. The most significant example from a Christian point of view is Judaism. But theistic beliefs are found among a wide variety of people (including many modern Europeans who own no ecclesiastical allegiance and who withhold assent to specifically Christian dogmas). Furthermore, although it is impossible to offer a rational demonstration of God's existence, the cosmological, teleological and moral arguments for theism have a hypothetical validity in so far as they show that if the data stated in their premises are to be ultimately intelligible we must postulate the existence of God the Creator. In these ways I differ from Barth. At the same time I gladly acknowledge his great contribution to Christian theology in many respects - chiefly in his affirmations of divine transcendence and in his emphasis on the supernatural character of Christian revelation. I am also indebted to him for illumination on many particular points of Christian doctrine.

2. The fundamental form of the division between theism and non-

theistic types of religious thought is that theists alone profess belief in a God who created the world 'out of nothing' and who is substantially distinct from it. Some modern theologians have blurred this difference and so imperilled the very foundations of Christianity. They have attempted to combine theism with Hegelian panentheism (according to which the world is the self-development of the Absolute) or with process thought (according to which God and the world create each other). The Tillichian definition of God as the 'ground' of our being is theologically dangerous because it is compatible with both theism and pantheism. It is the theistic affirmation of the Creator's ontological distinctness from all his creatures that distinguishes Christianity from Hinduism and makes a synthesis of the two religions impossible.

3. Christianity, as a special form of theism, is indissolubly linked to the doctrine of the Incarnation. By this doctrine I mean the belief that in one, and only one, person - Jesus of Nazareth - the Creator, without ceasing to be divine or mingling himself with our humanity, assumed a human nature 'for us men and for our salvation'. This doctrine determines the content of all other doctrines that Christians have held concerning God and his relation to mankind. In this century the doctrine has been endangered from two sides. On the one hand some theologians have misrepresented the doctrine by expounding it through non-theistic categories so that, first, Christ becomes no more than the supreme instance of God's general self-manifestation in the world and, secondly, the absolute uniqueness of the Incarnation therefore disappears. On the other hand other theologians, while starting from theistic premises, have regarded Christ as simply a perfect human creature who is the most adequate medium of God's self-revelation and saving activity. As (to take two examples from living memory) Bultmann's project of 'demythologization' and the publication of the symposium entitled *The Myth of God Incarnate* have shown, the fundamental question facing every Christian theologian, and indeed every Christian believer, is this. Was Jesus merely a man specially empowered by the Spirit to proclaim and enact a divine message or was he in his own person both human and divine?[3]

Finally I must state what I consider to be, first the nature of theistic statements, secondly the nature of doctrinal development and thirdly the place of doctrine, or dogma, in the Christian life.

Theistic statements are extremely varied; and a full examination of them would require an extensive discussion of religious language. Here I am concerned only to affirm my view of the basic statements that are contained in the doctrines I shall examine. These, I maintain, are to be interpreted objectively and ontologically. It is insufficient to regard them in a purely subjective manner, as indicating no more than the ways in which God appears to us or in which he affects our existence. They must be taken to signify his being in itself and as he has revealed itself to us. Otherwise we are ultimately condemned to complete agnosticism; so that the whole message of Christianity would be undermined. Yet they cannot be direct descriptions of divine reality; for God infinitely surpasses our understanding. They must be understood analogically. I have discussed and defended the theory of analogical predication in a book to which I have already referred.[4]

The question of doctrinal development is also a complex one on which I can here only give my opinion. My basic view is this. There is no one form of development. Sometimes (perhaps to a greater extent than is often recognized today) formal inferences are possible. I shall employ such inferences in the ensuing chapters. At other times, especially when calculations of historical probability are involved, we must have recourse to the kinds of informal inference that Newman so eloquently described. The overruling question, from the standpoint of distinctively Christian doctrine, is plainly this. What statements must we make in order to clarify and explicate the apostolic *depositum fidei* contained in the New Testament? There are no theological criteria for infallibly determining the answer to this question in any one case. All that a theologian can do is to exhibit the grounds and modes of his reasoning as fully as possible in the hope that they will be shared by his readers.

Thirdly, what is the place of dogma in the Christian life? During the last two hundred years or so there has been a widespread tendency among Christians to disparage dogma. What matters, it is said, is not assent to propositions concerning God but the experience of him and the practice of the charity that he commands. Obviously - and obvious though it ought to be it cannot be repeated too often (especially by theologians to themselves) - assent to dogma is insufficient. Assent (as I have said) is invalid unless it is based on experience. And neither assent nor experience are salvific unless they are permeated by love for God and man. If dogma is taken in isolation or even excessively emphasized it can stifle the soul. Yet without dogma experience and charity lack any specifically Christian grounding and direction. Religious experience can degenerate into some vague form of pantheistic feeling; and Christian charity can become indistinguishable from the concern that non-Christians, sometimes at the cost of herioc self-sacrifice, can show for their fellow-men. The experience and the charity of which the New Testament speaks were expressed in and formed by concrete beliefs concerning God and his revelation in Christ. These beliefs, in turn, were explicated by the early Church and authoritatively affirmed in its conciliar definitions.

A true estimation of dogma is especially required today when Christians are brought increasingly into contact with non-Christian religions, and when the Church is increasingly (and rightly) aware of its duty towards the oppressed and the poor. Let us first consider the relation between Christianity and other religions. The Christian experience of God has many elements in common with the experiences obtained by non-Christians. Thus Christianity, Judaism, Islam, Hinduism and Buddhism are all based on some kind of experience of an absolute reality transcending this world of space and time. Yet the

Christian kind differs from all other kinds in being shaped by distinctively Christian beliefs - above all, by those beliefs, firmly rooted in the New Testament, that were developed into the doctrines of the Incarnation, the Trinity and the Atonement. This fact is especially relevant to a consideration of mysticism. It is possible to draw up a list of characteristics that are shared by all those experiences that, by common consent, are called 'mystical'. Yet the experiences obtained by Christian mystics differ from those obtained by non-Christian mystics in so far as they are shaped by the distinctively Christian doctrines I have mentioned. And if this is true of mysticism it must *a fortiori* be true of those other forms of religious experience that mediate an apprehension of God with lesser intensity.

The same principle applies to Christian concern for social justice. Christians can unite with all men of good will in a recognition of human rights and in a determination to find a remedy for the ills unjustly endured by the poor and the oppressed. The specifically theistic reason for acknowledging human rights consists in the belief that God has made all men in his image and thus fashioned them for eternal life with him. The uniquely Christian reason is that God set such a value on us that he lived a human life and died a human death for our salvation. This reason is expressed in the Johannine writings by the affirmation, comprising the whole of social ethics, that we ought to love one another because God in Christ so loved us.[5]

---

[1] *The Christian Knowledge of God* (London 1969). In this book I have offered a general defence of theism from a philosophical viewpoint and with reference to philosophical objections.

[2] Immediately after I wrote the book mentioned above, T.F. Torrance's *Theological Science* (Oxford 1969) appeared. I am glad to take this opportunity of expressing my substantial agreement with him on basic points of religious epistemology. We both maintain that while Christian faith rests on an intuitive apprehension of divine reality it is wholly rational in terms of those propositions that are essential to it. Thus on the one hand Torrance affirms that all our knowledge of existent entities is based on an intuition which he defines as 'our apprehension of a reality in its objectivity and unity' (p 165), and that the truth claims of Christianity in particular are verified by a *sui generis* experience of God's self-revelation. On the other hand he insists that theological statements must be fully rational in a manner appropriate to the rationality inherent in their divine Object; so that theology 'must always be open for self-criticism in the face of new learning and reasonable argumentation on its own ground' (p282). Towards the end of his book (p 286) ff) Torrance states, in terms I find convincing, the epistemological similarities and differences between theology and the other sciences.

[3] I have examined Bultmann's theology in my *Revelation and Existence* (University of Wales Press, 1957). I have reviewed *The Myth of God Incarnate* in *Religious Studies* (13, pp 491-506); and I adhere to the criticisms I stated there. The value of this symposium, in my opinion, lies in its capacity to raise afresh two questions with which I shall deal later - is belief in the Incarnation essential to Christianity, and is there sufficient evidence in support of the belief? But, for the reasons that I state in my review, I do not think that the symposium provides adequate answers.

[4] *The Christian Knowledge of God* (especially pp 207 ff).

[5] Throughout this book I have taken it for granted that Christianity presupposes belief in God's objective reality. This presupposition has recently been challenged by a Cambridge theologian, Don Cupitt, in a book entitled *Taking Leave of God* (London 1980). Cupitt maintains that it is not necessary to believe that God exists, but that it is

sufficient to regard theistic statements as symbolizing spiritual ideals that we ought to achieve by our own unaided powers. Thus he writes that God is 'a unifying symbol that eloquently personifies and represents to us everything that spirituality requires of us' (p 9); that 'belief in the God of Christian faith is an expression of allegiance to a particular set of values, and experience of the God of Christian faith is experience of those values in one's life' (p 69); and that 'the religious requirement in itself is not a personal being but a categorical imperative principle' (p 94). Later he adds that God 'is not an actually existing individual person' but 'a humanly needed way of speaking generated by the impact of the religious demand and ideal upon us' (p 133). I offer three main observations on this view. First (as Cupitt admits on p 13) it represents a radical departure from tradition. From the N.T. onwards Christians have believed in God's independent reality.

This belief too has determined their whole understanding of worship, prayer and the spiritual life. Secondly, I fail to see why, on Cupitt's terms, 'God' is necessary even as a symbol (except perhaps in the initial stages of the spiritual way). All that finally matters is the set of spiritual values that 'God' symbolizes. Cupitt seems to admit this by affirming that even as a symbol or myth God is 'an "as if" whose spiritual value, great at first, thereafter diminishes' (p 107). Thirdly, Cupitt makes some statements implying that God does exist. Thus on p 82 he includes among his religious values 'receptivity to grace'. But can the latter exist if there is no personal God from whom grace is recieved? In his Preface Cupitt calls his account of religion 'Christian Buddhism'. It seems to me clear that he is invalidly attempting to fuse two entirely different types of religion - the one based on an autonomous form of spirituality and the other based on belief in the existence of a personal God on whose creative and redemptive will we totally depend. Admittedly the Christian can learn from Buddhist spirituality (as he can learn from the spirituality of other religions); for all spiritual truth proceeds from the one God who is omnipresent, drawing all men to himself; and very few Christians possess Christianity in a pure, ideal, form in which it does not need spiritual correction. Yet to admit this is one thing; but for a Christian to commit himself to a form of autonomous spirituality that implies virtual atheism is another.

CHAPTER 1
GOD THE CREATOR

The Christian doctrine of God is a complex one that can be approached from various standpoints. I have chosen to begin with the concept of creation. Before justifying my choice I shall offer a brief definition of the concept. I take it to signify three facts: that God makes the world 'out of nothing' (*ex nihilo*), that his creativity is continuous and that he is substantially distinct from the world.

First, then, God makes the world 'out of nothing' (*ex nihilo*). Everything that exists owes its existence wholly to him. Conversely, nothing whatsoever precedes his creative act. This act therefore differs in kind from, and is infinitely superior to, the work of any human creator. We speak, rightly, of the creativity shown by composers and artists. Yet they do not produce anything *ex nihilo*. However great their genius may be, it is limited to actualizing potentialities inherent in their given media - in a voice or instrument and in paint or stone. Similarly when two human parents pro-create a child they do so through the action of genetic material that they do not create.

Secondly, God's creativity is continuous. A literalistic interpretation of the creation-stories in Genesis can suggest that his creativity is limited to an initial moment of time that was 'the beginning' of the world. But by now it is widely recognized that these stories are to be taken, not as decriptions of historical events, but as symbolical statements of God's permanent relation to the world. God is the creator of everything at every moment of its existence. If he withdrew his creative presence from an entity for a second it would immediately cease to be. Although we find it natural to distinguish between creation and preservation they are in reality identical.

Thirdly, to say that God creates the world *ex nihilo* entails saying that he and the world are ontologically distinct. He does not produce the world by an extension of his being. The world is not simply himself in a reduced form. He creates it as something that is wholly other than him in its mode of being. Hence it is not, and cannot to the slightest degree become, divine. Even in mystical contemplation the human soul cannot become identical with God, however closely it may be united to him in love.

I have chosen the concept of creation as my starting-point for the following four reasons.

1. The concept clearly exemplifies the three main grounds for Christian belief in God: reason, revelation and experience. So far as reason is concerned it is enough to note that among the purely rational arguments for God's existence that are based on the nature of the world the fundamental one is the cosmological; for it is aimed at explaining, not merely this or that aspect of experience, but the very

existence of the world and of every item in it. My view of the argument
is this. On the one hand it does not prove God's existence with logical
certainty. On the other hand it is valid if it is put in the following
hypothetical form. The existence of any finite entity can be finally
explained only if it is attributed to the creative causality of a self-
existent Being who is ontologically distinct from the entities he creates.
And if he is the only final explanation of any finite entity he must be the
only final explanation of the world as a whole; for the whole is nothing
but the sum of such entities. Moreover, what is true of finite entities in
this world must, in this case, be true of such entities in any other world.
Yet a metaphysical hypothesis, even if it is required to make the world
finally intelligible, is an insufficient basis for faith. This basis is
provided by revelation and experience.

For Christians the earliest and doctrinally normative record of
divine revelation is contained in the Bible (especially the New
Testament). In several places the writers of the New Testament affirm
(and they nowhere deny) the concept of creation *ex nihilo*. Thus Paul
asserts in I Corinthians 8.6 that 'for us there is one God, the Father,
from whom are all things and for whom we exist, and one Lord Jesus
Christ though whom are all things and through whom we exist'. Again,
he says of the pre-existent Christ that 'in him all things were created, in
heaven and on earth, visible and invisible, whether thrones or
dominions or principalities or authorities - all things were created
through him and for him'.[1] Similarly the author of the fourth gospel
says of the divine Word who became flesh in Christ that 'all things were
made through him and without him was not anything made that was
made'.[2] So important did belief in God as the Creator become in the
early Church that it was stated at the beginning of the two creeds that
have been continually recited at public worship. The 'Apostles' creed
begins by professing belief in 'God the Father almighty, Maker of
heaven and earth'. The Nicene creed begins in almost exactly the same
way and adds the words 'and of all things visible and invisible'.

Belief in God the Creator rests finally on the experience of him as
one from whom we derive all that we are and can become.
Schleiermacher defined this experience as a feeling of absolute
dependence. Otto amplified the definition thus with reference to the
concept of creation. 'Desiring to give it a name of its own I propose to
call it creature-consciousness or creature-feeling. It is the emotion of a
creature, abased and overwhelmed by its own nothingness in contrast
to that which is supreme above all creatures.[3] Otto then proceeds to
show how this creature-consciousness expresses itself in the awareness
of God as the *mysterium tremendum*. The feeling of creaturely
dependence on God and the concomitant worship of him as the
Creator is perfectly summed up in Psalm 95 that has been incorporated
into Christian liturgy as the *Venite*. 'O come let us worship and bow
down, let us kneel before the Lord our Maker. For he is our God, and
we are the people of his pasture and the sheep of his hand.' Within
Christianity this religious attitude includes the worship of Christ as the

embodiment of the Creator's nature and the one on whom we totally depend for our salvation.

2. The concept of creation differentiates Christianity from non-Christian accounts of God's relation to the world.[4] Four main accounts can be discerned. First, there is the one given by Plato in his *Timaeus*. According to this God is the supreme Craftsman (*Demiourgos*). He does not create the world 'out of nothing'; he imposes form and order on unformed and disordered material that exists independently of him. Therefore he is not infinite or unconditioned Being. He is limited and conditioned both in his vision and in his action by, on the one hand the world of eternal Forms and, on the other, pre-existent matter. His task is to fashion out of the matter an imitation of and participation in the Forms. Although he may be called 'God' he is in fact no more than a super-human artist. Secondly, there is the view propounded by the Neo-Platonist Plotinus who held that the world is the last in a series of decreasingly real emanations from the One. The One did not create the world *ex nihilo*. Rather the world flows from the One in such a way that the latter's transcendence remains unimpaired.

The third non-Christian account of God's relation to the world is the one that has been most widely represented both in philosophy and in popular, non-philosophical accounts of religion. It goes by the name of pantheism or (in its less extreme mode) panentheism. According to pantheism God and the world are identical. According to panentheism although God transcends the world in one part of his being he also communicates another part to it. According to both views, therefore, the world is divine in so far as it is the self-expression of God's nature. In the ancient world Stoicism was the most influential type of pantheistic philosophy. In the modern world the seventeenth-century philosopher Spinoza represents pantheism in its purest form. He held that everything in the world is a mode of God under one of his two attributes of thought or extension. A more dynamic interpretation of pantheism (or at least panentheism) was given in the nineteenth century by Hegel for whom history was the self-development of God (or the Absolute) in ways that the human mind can rationally articulate.

Fourthly, there is process thought. This is a twentieth century system of philosophical theology that was originated by A.N. Whitehead and has been developed by Charles Hartshorne. It has an affinity with Plato's cosmology in so far as it represents God as introducing structure and meaning into an antecedently existing flux that he did not create. But its exponents go beyond Plato in distinguishing between two aspects of God and by affirming that in one of his aspects God changes through his response to the world. In his 'primordial' nature God exists eternally and immutably apart from the world. In his 'consequent' nature he is constantly changing, constantly growing in perfection and so surpassing himself, by including within himself the world's experiences. Hence at the end of

Process and Reality Whitehead writes that 'it is as true to say that God transcends the world as that the world transcends God' and that 'it is as true to say that God creates the world as that the world creates God'.

3. We can deduce other divine properties from the concept of creation. If God is the Creator he must be personal, omnipotent, omniscient, self-existent, necessary, eternal, immutable and good.

First, the Creator must be personal; for the act of creation is an act of will. Here there is a difference between theism and many other views of God or the Absolute. According to Plotinus the One from which everything emanates is supra-personal. No properties can be ascribed to it. The very idea of emanation (with its suggestion of a ray proceeding from the sun) is non-personal. Similarly many pantheistic or monistic forms of religion or religious philosophy imply a non-personal view of God. Obviously if pantheism is taken in its strict sense to signify an identity between God and the world God must be impersonal to the extent that he is identical with impersonal processes. The non-personal character of the monist's Absolute emerges with special clarity in those Hindu writings that describe *Brahman* as a reality to which all human categories are inapplicable. But any act of making implies a maker, and a maker must be personal.

Also the Creator must be omnipotent and omniscient. He must be omnipotent in the two senses that this world can bear. If he is able to bring something into being out of nothing he must be capable of doing anything that is in accordance with his nature and will. Equally he must be sovereign over, and so be in complete control of, all he has created. He must too be omniscient. He must have a perfect knowledge of all his creatures; for the latter are simply projections of ideas that pre-exist in his mind. I shall examine the modes of God's sovereignty and omniscience in chapter four.

If God is the Creator he must also be self-existent and self-sufficient. In other words he must exist 'from himself' (*a se*). Theologians have constantly distinguished between God and all creatures by affirming that although both he and they exist by or in themselves (*per se*) only he exists *a se*. Thus while a man exists 'in himself' in so far as he is distinct from other persons and things he does not exist 'from himself'; he is not self-existent or self-sufficient; he depends for his existence on innumerable finite factors, and ultimately on God. However, if God is the Creator he must exist *a se*. The idea of *aseitas* is entailed by the idea of creativity. The alternative to saying that God exists solely from resources interior to his being is to say that he was created by someone else so that the latter and not he would then be the Creator.

At this point it may be said that the same being could be both created and creator. There might be a God who is wholly uncreated but who chose to create the world through another being whom he created. This view (which was held by Arius) has been continually rejected by orthodox theologians who have argued that the New Testament's attribution of a creative function to Christ the Son implies his consubstantiality with the uncreated Father. The argument is invincible. To be created *ex nihilo* - to be totally and incessantly dependent on another - excludes the capacity to create *ex nihilo*. In any case if God could create through a created intermediary he alone would be *the* Creator, the ultimate Source of all things.

Furthermore from the fact that God is the Creator it is possible to infer that he is necessary and eternal. There are two forms of ontological necessity. There is the relative form by which finite beings exist through the action of causes external to themselves; and there is the absolute form by which God exists through an internal power of his own being. The belief that God exists by the second form of necessity is entailed by belief in his self-existence (or *aseitas*). The test of the entailment is this. If the person we call 'God', and worship as such, does not exist by a necessity of his own being he might not have existed; but if he might not have existed he might have been produced by a higher being who would then be the Creator and the one who is worthy of adoration. Hence unless the person we call 'God' exists necessarily we cannot *know* that he is the Creator of all things. This conclusion is supported by the cosmological argument that, according to Aquinas's Third Way, terminates in the postulation of God as the necessary ground of contingent being. And if God exists necessarily he must be eternal at least in so far as he is without beginning or end.

If God is the Creator he must also be immutable in the sense that he cannot change in any of his properties. He cannot be thus changed either by a higher being (for there is no such being) or by his creatures (for they are totally dependent on and distinct from him). Moreover, if he exists necessarily he must actualize all his properties simultaneously; for in any entity existence and essence - *that* an entity is and *what* it is — are, though notionally distinguishable, ontologically inseparable. This entailment of God's immutability by his necessity can be put thus. If God could change in any of his attributes he could change in all of them. Also if he could change by the increase of an attribute he could also change by the decrease of one. We cannot set limits to contingency. But if God could decrease in some of his attributes he could decrease in all of them; and so, eventually, he could pass out of existence altogether.[5]

Finally, the Creator must be good. If God were wholly evil we could not explain the presence of goodness in his creatures. Also if he were wholly evil we should be compelled to affirm that unless his creation of the world was motiveless he created it out of sheer malevolence. Yet does not the fact that we are evil as well as good compel us to attribute evil as well as goodness to God? It does not do so for the following reasons. Evil is teleologically as well as (what is true by definition) morally wrong because it thwarts the end or goal (*telos*) of human nature. The only alternative to admitting this is to pursue evil in the place of good for the sake of personal fulfilment. Therefore if there is a God, evil must be contrary to his purpose in creating us. Of course the problem of evil remains, and I shall discuss it later.

The divine attributes I have mentioned can also be inferred from the religious attitudes that the theist adopts towards God as the Creator. Especially they can be inferred from prayer, worship and the trust that worshippers place in God's providence. We could not pray to God unless he were personal. He would not be worthy of adoration unless he were good. We could not trust him and commit ourselves wholly to him unless he were also omnipotent, omniscient, eternal and immutable in wisdom, power and love. Again, prayer, worship and trust imply that God is the *ultimate* reality (so that he exists *a se*), and that he is indestructible (so that he exists necessarily). Admittedly theists do not normally arrive at belief in God's attributes through any kind of inference. They obtain the belief on the authority of a tradition that they find confirmed in varying degrees by their own experience. Nevertheless, the inferences I have stated articulate the creeds' primary affirmation of belief in God as 'the Maker of all things'; so that, if asked, the believer would say that it is inconceivable that the Creator should not possess these attributes.

4. The concept of creation also entails further assertions concerning God's relation to the world. Among these the following are particularly important.

First, if God is the Creator he must be transcendent in three ways.

(a) He must be transcendent in the sense of being the sole and ontologically distinct ground of the world's existence. The fact that he is its sole ground differentiates him from Plato's *Demiourgos* and Whitehead's God who both act on independently given material. The fact that he is ontologically distinct from the world differentiates him from the God in whom pantheists and panentheists believe. Belief in his distinctness is entailed by belief in his creativity; for one who brings entities into being *ex nihilo* is necessarily distinct from them. Belief in God's distinctness is also entailed by belief in his personality. Every human person is distinct from every other person. No one can merge himself with someone else even when he is united to another person by the closest ties of love. Ontological incommunicability belongs to the essence of selfhood.

(b) God is transcendent in his mode of being. This form of transcendence is expressed by saying that he is infinite. The 'in' here has the force of a negative prefix. It means that God is free from all those limitations that characterize creatures. His infinity is indicated by most of the attributes that I have deduced from his creativity - by his omnipotence, omniscience and aseity. Even those attributes that do not immediately suggest his infinity must be qualified by the words 'infinite' and 'infinitely' if anthropomorphism is to be avoided. Thus God is infinitely personal and infinitely good. The infinite character of the ways in which he possesses these properties is shown in his creativity; but it is supremely shown by Christian revelation through which we learn that his personality takes a triune form (to which there is no finite parallel) and that his love for us led him to live a human life and undergo a human death.

(c) Because God transcends us in the order of being he also transcends us in the order of knowing. No finite mind can comprehend him in his essence, as he is *per se*. His capacity to create *ex nihilo* is itself incomprehensible. Its incomprehensibility is stated thus by the second Isaiah. 'To whom, then, will you compare me, that I should be like him? says the Holy One. Lift up your eyes on high and see: who created these? He who brings out their host by number, calling them all by name; by the greatness of his might and because he is strong in power not one is missing.'[6] Obviously too we cannot understand those attributes that are entailed by belief in God's creativity. We cannot hope to understand them by extending indefinitely their finite modes of instantiation; for such an extension would result in the absurd idea of God as a magnified man.

Yet, secondly, the idea of God's creativity implies that he is immanent as well as transcendent. He did not make the world 'at the beginning' and then withdraw his contact with it. He is continuously present in it by his creative power. Moreover, if he creates it *ex nihilo* this power must affect every aspect of every being; it must be omnipresent. God must therefore always be nearer to each of his creatures than any of them can be to each other. The realization of his incomparable nearness is a constantly recurring element in religious experience.

However, the concept of immanence can imply diluted pantheism. It can suggest that God indwells the world in a quasi-local manner, as a man dwells in a house. Yet this is a thoroughly incoherent notion. It is incompatible with two of the divine properties I have mentioned: infinity and personality. Infinite and uncreated Being cannot compress itself within the limits of entities that are finite and created, any more than a gallon of water can be poured into a vessel made to contain only a pint. Also the idea that God infuses himself into creatures is incompatible with the ascription of personality to him. Selfhood, as I have said, is incommunicable. Thus, however much a husband may love, sympathize with and intuitively understand his wife he cannot impart his personality to her. A basic condition of love and sympathy is that the one who loves and sympathizes is distinct from the one who is loved and with whom sympathy is felt.

When, therefore, we speak of God's immanence we must discard the physicalistic associations of the term and resist the temptation to think of him as actually imparting himself to those beings whom he created. His immanence is not something additional to his creativity; it is simply his creative causality in so far as this affects his creatures. This point was made with characteristic precision by Aquinas when he wrote that 'God exists in everything, not indeed as part of their substance or as an accident, but as an agent is present to that in which its action is taking place'.[7] In order to avoid the pantheistic implications of 'immanence' it may be thought desirable to speak of God's presence 'to' rather than of his presence 'in' his creatures. Yet no form of words can enable us to understand God's immanence which is as mysterious as his transcendence. Just as there is no finite parallel to his transcendent power in creating something out of nothing so there is no parallel to the universality and depth of the mode in which he is present in (or to) his creatures without merging himself with them. As with everything that concerns God's being and activity we can only affirm a mystery and give grounds for the affirmation. We cannot unravel the mystery and explain it.

In order to maintain belief in God the Creator and so all subsequent beliefs concerning our relation to him it is necessary to affirm his transcendence and his immanence equally. An excessive, deistic, emphasis on his transcendence removes him from control of and care for the universe. It thereby undermines belief in his providence and in the efficacy of petitionary prayer. An excessive emphasis on his immanence can produce incipient pantheism. In the classical forms of the Judaeo-Christian tradition God's transcendence and immanence have been stressed equally as two aspects of one reality. Thus although the Old Testament affirms the transcendent majesty of God it also affirms his omnipresence as the Creator. These affirmations are both made magnificently in Psalm 139. An equal awareness of God's transcendence and immanence characterizes Christian mysticism of which E. L. Mascall writes as follows. 'For the transcendent God who is sought in the cloud of unknowing is present already in the depth of the soul; while the immanent God who dwells in the centre of our being is infinite, perfect and self-existent.'[8]

Thirdly, because God is related to the world as Creator to created there is a likeness as well as an unlikeness between them. Yet we must state the likeness with care. We cannot infer it simply from the premise 'every effect is like its cause'. Some causes are unlike their effects. Thus the striking of a match is unlike the flame it produces. In any case the relation between God and the world cannot be expressed as an instance of a principle governing the relation between one creature and another. The claim that God's created effects resemble him must be based on his absolute uniqueness as the Creator. And the claim is this. Because God creates the world *ex nihilo* there is nothing external to him to which he must conform himself. Everything that exists is a finite embodiment of an idea that pre-exists in his mind. Therefore the world must be an imitation of his nature, a projection into finitude of his infinite perfection. Here there is a complete difference between God and a human 'creative' artist. Every such artist creates out of a material that is given to him and that limits the degree of his self-expression. Even a highly gifted poet's powers of imagination are restricted by the world of his experience. The maxim *nihil in intellectu quod non prius in sensu* is of universal application in the finite sphere. We cannot imagine or conceive anything of which we have not formed a notion through our sense-impressions. With God it is wholly otherwise. He knows only himself and the world in so far as it is an expression of himself.[9]

The fact that there is a likeness as well as an unlikeness between God and his creatures can be expressed by saying that there is an analogy of being (*analogia entis*) between them. Because of this analogy it is possible to predicate finite properties of God 'by analogy'. There are various forms of analogical predication; but the form I now have in mind and that corresponds to the analogy of being is the analogy of proportionality. Its essence is this. When we say (to take an obvious example) that God is wise we ought not to predicate wisdom of him univocally (that is, in the same sense in which we predicate wisdom of a man); for such a mode of predication would represent him anthropomorphically. Yet we cannot predicate wisdom of him equivocally (that is, in a sense that is totally different from the sense in which we predicate wisdom of a man); for such a mode of predication would be non-significant. The analogy of proportionality constitutes a mean between these two extremes. It enables us to assert, according to the combination of likeness and unlikeness between the Creator and his creatures, that just as a man is wise in a form proportional to his human nature so God is wise in a manner proportional to his divine nature. The one is wise humanly; the other is wise divinely.

Obviously the higher a creature is on the scale of being the more it resembles its Creator. On the terrestrial plane the highest form of being is man. In terms of his rationality, capacity for voluntary action and self-consciousness he alone is entitled to be called personal and spiritual. He alone, therefore, reflects the personality and spirituality of the Creator. The Bible states his distinctiveness on this score by affirming that he alone bears God's image. Other creatures are like God in some of their properties. Thus a rock is like him in its durability and its capacity to afford shelter in a storm. Yet only man is like God in his essence - by reason of his distinctive nature as a person. Hence we can attribute personal properties to God with a special appropriateness. He is our Father, Lord, Saviour and Friend. Of course we must qualify all these terms when we apply them to God. Yet when we qualify them we do not mean, if we are true to Biblical theism, that God is non-personal. We mean that he possesses in an infinite mode properties that we possess in finite modes.

A co-incidence of approaches is discernible here. Just as the idea of creation implies the idea of a personal Creator who possesses personal properties, so the same idea compels us to affirm that the greatest possible degree of likeness to the Creator must be exhibited by the highest, most developed, members of the created realm. Yet may not God also possess supra-personal properties to which there are no created analogues? I do not see any purely rational way of disproving the possibility; but I offer two comments. First, to say that God may be supra-personal is to use words without meaning. We cannot conceive any form of being that is intrinsically higher than the personal form we know, with absolute immediacy, in ourselves. The idea of a supra-personal God is logically akin to Locke's idea of substance; it is a 'something I know not what' that as such is meaningless. My second reason for rejecting the idea of a supra-personal God takes us beyond natural theology. It is that God has revealed himself in Christ as one who is essentially personal - as one who does not and cannot exceed his nature as Father, Son and Holy Spirit.

There is yet another way in which belief in God as the Creator determines our understanding of his relation to the world. If the world depends continuously on him it is not a 'closed system' that can operate only within those limits and according to those laws that it originally acquired. It must be constantly open to such new effects as God may choose to cause in it. It must possess (to use a scholastic phrase) an obedient potency (*potentia obedientialis*) in relation to God's actions. Christians believe that God has acted supernaturally on the created order in three main ways: in the Incarnation by which he united a human nature to his own, in communicating Christ's life to believers through the Holy Spirit and in miracles (chiefly the Resurrection). I shall discuss the first and second of these ways at length in subsequent chapters. Here I shall state the nature of the miraculous and consider some of the problems connected with it.

I shall define a miracle as 'an unusual event of a physical or material kind that supersedes the laws of nature and is due to a supernatural act of God'. This definition raises three main problems.

1. It has frequently been objected that miracles are impossible because they conflict with the laws of nature. Much depends on how we interpret the latter. Two interpretations are possible. According to the first the laws merely state the ways in which nature *in fact* behaves. According to the second the laws state the ways in which nature *must* behave. Let us take the statement 'If A occurs B will occur'. According to the first interpretation this statement merely records a regular sequence of events. It is simply a fact of experience that A is always followed by B. According to the second interpretation the statement affirms a natural necessity. A is so constituted that it *must* be followed by B. The same difference of interpretation correspondingly affects our understanding of the converse statement 'If B occurs A has occurred'.

I do not here propose to debate these two interpretations on their intrinsic merits. My sole aim is to consider their compatibility or incompatibility with the idea of the miraculous. The first is obviously compatible. If the relation between A and B is merely one of sequence there is no good reason why the sequence should not be broken. Correspondingly there is no good reason why the laws that state these sequences should not have exceptions. The only reason that can be given is the principle of natural uniformity. However this principle is notoriously unprovable. If there is no necessary connexion between A and B we cannot prove either that because B normally follows A it must always follow it or that because A normally precedes B it must always precede it. Even if we could be absolutely sure that in every instance A and B have been thus related in the past we should have no grounds for affirming that they must be similarly related in the future.

A *prima facie* case against the possibility of miracles is much stronger if we regard physical laws as signifying objective necessities in nature. Yet the case is answerable. A physical law is formulated on the supposition that no supernatural factors operate. Hence if they operate the law is inapplicable during the time of their operation. Hence too causal necessities covered by the law are annulled. Moreover, the concept of creation entitles us to affirm that this form of supernatural intervention in nature is possible. If there are natural necessities they, like everything else in the created realm, are God-given. Like everything else in nature, therefore, they have only a relative independence or derived autonomy. They act so long as God wills that they act, just as the entities they characterize exist so long as God wills that they exist. Having created them God can suspend them and replace them with new powers. Whether he has done so is another question. The question is a double one and embraces the second and third problems.

2. Can we ever be sure that an event is scientifically inexplicable and so is entitled to be called a miracle? It is well known that some events that at one time seem to be inexplicable are at a later time found to be explicable in terms of further scientific investigation. Thus to a medieval man all kinds of technological achievement that we take for granted would have seemed impossible. Is it not then rash to say of any abnormal event that it can never be explained in terms of natural powers and so brought within the scope of natural law either through the modification of an old law or through the introduction of a new one? Ought we not always to retain an open mind concerning every unusual event, however astonishing it may be?

It is certainly tempting to give affirmative answers to these questions and so to exclude miracles from consideration. Yet if we did so we should be carrying agnosticism too far. It is possible to specify some occurrences that fall outside the scope of existing laws and correlative experience to such an extent that our whole understanding of the world would be undermined if they could be attributed to natural powers. Such an occurrence would be the resurrection of Christ as this is recorded in the New Testament. Can we entertain the idea that dead bodies have hitherto undiscovered properties that enable them to leave their tombs and re-appear in transfigured modes to the living? We cannot do so without calling in question everything that has been scientifically established concerning the human organism.

3. What are the criteria for establishing that a miracle has occurred? The main ones, I suggest, are these. (i) We have no right to believe in a miracle unless the evidence for it survives the most rigorous scrutiny. We have no right to do so for two reasons. First, our whole lives are governed by the presupposition of natural uniformity. We could not live with any confidence unless we assumed in countless cases that B will follow A in the future as it has done in the past. Secondly our whole trust in God implies the belief that his governance of nature is reliable. The religious person is bound to assume that if God suspends the laws

of nature he does so only on rare occasions for a special purpose. (ii) No one has a right to believe that an event has been miraculously caused unless it is congruous with God's nature and will. There are also two subordinate criteria. The case for a supposed miracle is strengthened in proportion (iii) to the trustworthiness of the eye-witnesses and (iv) to the impact of the miracle on their lives. Admittedly in the light of these criteria the case for many miracles is very weak. Yet if we grant that miracles are possible there is no *a priori* reason for affirming that a convincing case is never available. Admittedly too these criteria cannot be used to prove that a miracle has occurred. Even when they are fully satisfied the attribution of an event to the supernatural activity of God and so its designation as a miracle require a distinctive act of spiritual intuition. However such an act is always required for the apprehension of God's existence and activity.

I have maintained that on both historical and theological grounds the doctrine of creation can be regarded as the basis of Christian theology. I shall now state two complementary truths concerning the doctrine and then consider God's purpose in creating the world. The truths are these. On the one hand God's act in creating the world and his motive in creating it are mysteries that no human mind can comprehend. On the other hand although they are thus supra-rational they are not irrational.

First, God's act of creating the world is a mystery. There is no finite parallel to creation *ex nihilo* or to the manner in which God indwells his creatures. Hence we cannot comprehend God's creativity. *A fortiori* we cannot comprehend his *aseitas* and self-existence from which his creativity proceeds. Kant wrote impressively of this in the following words that convey, in a philosophical mode, a 'sense of the numinous'. 'Unconditional necessity which, as the ultimate support and stay of all existing things, is an indispensable requirement of the mind, is an abyss on the verge of which human reason trembles in dismay. Even the idea of eternity, terrible and sublime as it is, does not produce upon the mental vision such a feeling of awe and terror; for, although it *measures* the duration of things it does not *support* them.'[10]

Yet although God's creativity and *aseitas* are supra-rational, belief in them is not irrational. On the contrary although we cannot comprehend them we can understand that they represent in infinite and absolute modes forms of personal being and activity that we possess only in finite and relative modes. If we can partially create through actualizing the potentialities of given matter it is reasonable to believe in a God who can create *ex nihilo*. Again, if we are partially independent of our background and environment we can reasonably believe that God is wholly independent of everything. The same principle can be applied to the concepts of power and knowledge. If we are able to do some of the things that lie within the scope of human nature we can reasonably postulate the existence of a God who can do everything that is in accordance with divine nature. And if we are able to know some of the things that are knowable we can reasonably postulate the existence of a God who can know everything that is knowable. Throughout we posit a divine activity that, so far from being incompatible with finite activities, is their infinite completion.

The same complementary truths emerge from a consideration of God's motive in creating the world. God, being self-sufficient, does not need anyone or anything. Hence if he is good his motive for creating the world must be pure generosity. In other words he must be motivated by a form of love that is wholly altruistic. This too is a mystery. There is no finite parallel to love without need. Even when a human person performs altruistic acts of love they still minister to his needs in the sense that if he did not perform them he would not be fully human. On the human plane charity is a necessary form of self-realization. God, however, would be fully divine even if he had not created a world on which he bestows his love.

Yet the attribution of creative love to God is not irrational. It conforms to the same principle that operates in the attribution of creative power to him. Although we cannot comprehend such love we can rationally postulate it because we can understand it sufficiently to see that it constitutes an absolute mode of a spirituality that we can exhibit only in finite modes. Infinite love is not incompatible with finite love. On the contrary it fulfils all that finite love at its best contains. It constitutes a pure expression of an altruism that human acts can only partially exemplify.

However, to say that God does not need the world does not imply that he does not delight in it. On the contrary he is bound to delight in it if he is its Creator, and if he is love. Here we must proceed by analogy with the created order. If even human creators delight in the limited works they create, how much more must God delight in the universe that he creates *ex nihilo.* Also if we delight in what we love how much more must God delight in what he loves with complete selflessness. We can bring creativity and love together in the form of the following analogical inference. If two parents delight in a child whom they procreate as the result of a love for each other that is indistinguishable from their need of each other, how much more must God delight in a world that he created out of an absolutely pure love from which all need is absent.

A consideration of God's motive in creating leads to the following question. Is God's act in creating free or necessary? It is both in ways appropriate to his infinite being. It is free in so far as he is not obliged to create through any external constraint or in order to fulfil his nature. But it is not free in the sense that he could have chosen not to create. Similarly it is not necessary in the sense that without it his nature would be incomplete. But it is necessary in so far as it is a necessary expression of his nature. If God exists *a se* all his acts must constitute an inevitable and wholly adequate expression of his being; they must take the form of a spontaneous overflowing into finitude of what he is infinitely within himself. The same truth can be approached by the type of analogical reasoning I have already employed. Even on the human plane acts of love are, ideally, spontaneous; they are, ideally, the necessary expression of the agent's goodness. To say that a person is free not to perform such an act is to say that he is free to sin (either negatively through refraining from the act when it is within his power or positively by performing an unloving act). The 'perfect freedom' at which we ought to aim is not the ability not to love but the inability to do anything that does not exhibit love. Hence to deny spontaneity to God's creative love is to deny that he reaches even the ideal that is set for his creatures. Yet the difference between God and his creatures remains. Only he, as self-existent Being, can by a necessity of his own nature perform an act of love that adds nothing to his own perfection but is performed solely for the benefit of others.

What I have said concerning God's creative love is not merely a piece of abstract speculation. It affects the very basis of religion. This basis is worship. Now worship implies, first, that God is our Creator and, secondly, that he does not merely exemplify human ideals but also surpasses them as *id quo nihil maius cogitari potest* (that than which nothing greater can be conceived). Surely nothing greater can be conceived than the love of a God who created the world although he had no need of it at all.

What, then, was God's purpose in creating the world? The answer to this question emerges from what I have already said. If his motive in creating it was self-diffusing goodness (or altruistic love) his only purpose could have been to reproduce his glory and perfection in his creatures. Every creature reflects this glory to some degree; each is a finite imitation of the Creator. But among terrestrial creatures man is the only bearer of God's image. He alone possesses the spirituality that makes him in his essence like God. Of course we must avoid anthropocentrism. God delights in sub-human creatures; and the fact that he made them out of love is the final reason why we should respect them (especially those that are sentient). Also there may be creatures (such as angels) who are spiritually superior to us. Nevertheless even if such creatures exist they differ from us in degree, not in kind; so that what applies to us must apply also to them in a higher form. In any case we can speak with certainty only of our own world. Within this world man is the crown of the evolutionary process and is unique in the mode of his resemblance to the Creator.

God's purpose for man is fivefold.

1. Although man is compounded of both mind and body, spirit and matter, his distinctive role in the order of creation is to develop his spiritual faculties of intellect, will and love. Certainly his bodily nature also reflects God's glory. Yet it does so only to the extent that it is governed and permeated by his spirit.

2. Man's spirituality is fulfilled only in communion with God. Among man's highest gifts is the gift of self-consciousness. On the religious

level this means that although other creatures reflect God unconsciously only man can be aware of himself as a creature and enjoy communion with God. Hence this communion is his supreme glory and the final end of his existence.

3. This communion too is meant to be eternal. God, as infinite love, desires the highest good for all his creatures. The highest good for a spiritual creature is that his relationship with God should be endless. Hence the idea of creation implies the idea of immortality. If man perished like the brutes his spiritual potentialities would be frustrated. And God's generosity would thereby be limited.

4. Both in this life and in the next man can have no nobler activity than the adoration and praise of God. Here there has been much misunderstanding. In glorifying God we are not submitting to a self-opinionated despot who demands our flattery. On the contrary we are fulfilling our own natures by recognizing them for what they are - splintered reflections of their divine Archetype who out of pure love has made us for fellowship with him.

5. All theists can agree on these four propositions. But Christians further believe that God has fully and finally revealed his purpose for mankind in Christ. God's purpose for every man is that he should become like Christ by being united with Christ through the Holy Spirit. Through this union believers become members of God's Kingdom and obtain even within this world of space and time a life that is eternal.

Thus the concept of creation brings us to the threshold of distinctively Christian faith. In the concluding section of this chapter I shall indicate ways in which the concept is relevant to the three basic Christian doctrines of the Incarnation, the Trinity and the Atonement.

Both Jews and Christians believe in God as the Creator. Christians, however, further believe that God exists in the triune form of Father, Son and Holy Spirit, and that God the Son became man in Christ for their salvation. To the doctrine of creation Christians add the doctrines of the Incarnation, the Trinity and the Atonement. These doctrines cannot be deduced from the doctrine of creation. They were developed in the light of a new revelation of God in Christ. Yet they imply the doctrine of creation and cannot be understood apart from it.

Belief in God as the Creator determines the traditional understanding of the Incarnation. In modern times the latter has been interpreted in terms of various views concerning God and his relation to the world. But in the ancient Church it was always interpreted in terms of the contrast between the Creator and his creatures. This contrast (that Athanasius significantly placed at the beginning of his *De Incarnatione*) underlay the whole dispute between Arius and his orthodox opponents. Whereas Arius held that Christ was merely a creature the first council of Nicaea held that he fully shared the uncreated being of God. The same contrast is presupposed by the

Chalcedonian Definition's later affirmation that although Christ was constituted by an indivisible and inseparable union of a divine nature with a human nature in the person of the Son the natures were unconfused and unchanged. The last two adjectives were required by the assumption that the immortal Creator cannot mingle his being with or change it into the being of a mortal creature.

Those who do not base their christology on the concept of creation *ex nihilo* inevitably exhibit Christ as one who differs in degree, but not in kind, from other men. Thus according to Hegelianism Christ can be no more than the supreme expression of God's universal presence in humanity. Again, for Whitehead Christ can be no more than the moment of greatest significance in the cosmic process whereby God and the world create each other. By contrast those who follow the teaching of the councils are obliged to hold that although no man is divine God in Christ totally transcended his normal relation to creatures by hypostatically uniting a human nature to his own. It is only if we place Christ in the context of the Creator-creature relationship that we can regard him as being absolutely unique and intrinsically unsurpassable.

It may not appear at first sight that belief in God as the Creator is relevant to the doctrine of the Trinity. Yet I suggest two major points at which its relevance can be shown.

1. The idea of creation involves the following antinomy. On the one hand God is self-sufficient; he is perfect without the world of which he has no need. On the other hand if he is perfect in personality he must also be perfect in love; but love implies an object of love that is external to the lover; and so God cannot be self-sufficient. I doubt whether pure reason can resolve this antinomy. At any rate it is resolved by the doctrine of the Trinity according to which God enjoys an infinite life of love within himself through the mutual indwelling of the Father, the Son, and the Holy Spirit.

2. If man is made in God's image and if God is triune we must expect to discover signs of his triunity in his creatures. Many created analogies of the Trinity have been suggested. They are usually divided into two classes: psychological analogies and social ones. According to the first class the Trinity is likened to various faculties of the human soul that, though distinct, interpenetrate so as to form one entity. According to the second class the Trinity is likened to a society of human persons who are joined to each other by a union of love. I cannot examine these analogies here. I am concerned only to state the basic principle that although both types of analogy have defects both signify the truth that human creatures are finite and imperfect copies of a unity-in-diversity that is found infinitely and perfectly in the Creator.

The concept of creation is also relevant to our understanding of the doctrine of the Atonement. The essence of the doctrine is best approached through etymology. Atonement means, literally, at-one-ment. To atone therefore means to set at one, to unite, to reconcile.

Through sin we are estranged from God. Christ reconciles us to God and so makes us at one with him. This act of atonement is supernatural in two respects. It is effected by the supernatural act of the Incarnation. Also it enables us to participate in the life of Christ as the incarnate Lord and so to achieve a supernatural mode of perfection. Yet although it thus exceeds anything that can be accomplished through the natural order of creation it also fulfils this order in the following ways. First, the Christ by whom we are redeemed is the incarnation of the eternal Word by whom we were created. Secondly, although Christ was fully divine he was also fully human. As man he possessed, as we do, a created nature. And we are redeemed as much by his humanity as by his deity. Thirdly, the perfection that Christians achieve through their union with Christ does not suppress any of their created faculties. Rather it confers on these faculties new powers. Grace (to quote a maxim that can scarcely be too often repeated) perfects, not destroys, nature.

¹ Col. 1.16.

² Jn. 1.3.

³ *The Idea of the Holy* (Oxford 1923, p 10).

⁴ I have devoted another book solely to an examination of theism in relation to non-theistic systems of religious thought (*Concepts of Deity,* London 1971).

⁵ The attribute of divine immutability acutely exemplifies the difference between the theistic belief in God as the Creator and other accounts of God's relation to the world. Thus, according to process thought, God *must* change through his absorption of the world's exeriences. Similarly, according to pantheism, God *must* change through modifications of his being by cosmic events. However, according to theism God, *qua* the Creator, *cannot* be changed by the world. No creature, *qua* creature, can either add to or subtract from his perfection. Hence while it is true to say that God fulfils his purpose in history it is not true to say that he fulfils *himself* or in any sense becomes what he was not before this historical fulfilment. I cannot attach any sense to Pannenberg's assertion that 'the futurity of God's rule implies that in some sense the *existence* of God himself is yet future'. (I take this quotation from E.F. Tupper's *The Theology of Wolfhart Pannenberg,* London 1974, p 199. Tupper quotes other sentences to the same effect). The theistic affirmation of God's sovereignty implies that, in both his *aseitas* and the properties that characterize it, he remains the same at every point of the world's history.

⁶ Is. 40. 25-6.

⁷ S.T. 1a 8. 1.

⁸ *He Who Is* (London 1945, p 143).

⁹ O. C. Quick put it thus. 'When we are thinking of God, there is no longer any distinction possible between what his work reveals or displays, and what it expresses of his own mind and nature. For what God creates, he does not make out of any material which he finds existing outside himself. All things depend for their being on him, the creator of all. And, since he creates out of the infinite resources of his own being, all things in various manners and degrees of perfection express him'. *(Doctrines of the Creed,* London 1968, pp 54-5). Cf. E.L. Mascall's *Existence and Analogy* (London 1949, pp 122-3). It seems to me clear that unless there were an analogy of being - a likeness as well as an unlikeness - between creatures and their Creator we should not have any basis for attributing positive concepts and images to God; for the only meaning we can attach to any of these is the one derived from its instantiation in finite being. Hence Brunner was right in maintaining against Barth that the *analogia entis,* so far from being something distinctively Roman Catholic, is a presupposition of all theological discourse *(Natural Theology,* London 1946, pp 54-6). As the result of careful analysis B. Mondin concludes that Barth's two main objections to the *analogia entis* are, first, that it eliminates the qualitative difference between God and man by including them under the same genus of

'being', and, secondly, that it starts with man and ascends to God instead of starting with God and descending to man *(The Principle of Analogy in Protestant and Catholic Theology,* The Hague, 1963, p 168). Neither of these objections is valid. The doctrine of creation requires us to affirm that God's form of being is qualitatively different from the form possessed by any created entity. Also, although God is prior in the order of being, man is prior in the order of knowing in so far as we can attribute perfections to God only by analogy with their embodiment in his creatures. Thus, although (as Ephesians 3, 14-15 affirms) God's fatherhood is the archetype of human fatherhood, we can meaningfully speak of the former only in terms of the latter.

[10] *Critique of Pure Reason* (Transcendental Dialectic, 2.3.5.)

CHAPTER 2
GOD INCARNATE

My aim in this chapter is to state the doctrine of the Incarnation, to assess its Biblical grounds and then to examine its classical formulations. The basis of the doctrine is contained in two documents produced by the ancient church: the prologue to the fourth gospel and the Nicene creed.

Verses 1-3 of the Johannine prologue run thus. 'In the beginning was the Word, and the Word was with God and the Word was God. He was in the beginning with God; all things were made through him, and without him was not anything made that was made.' According to verse 14 this divine and creative Word became man in Christ. 'And the Word became flesh and dwelt among us, full of grace and truth; we have beheld his glory, glory as of the only Son from the Father.' 'Flesh' here signifies, not merely the matter of which our bodies are composed, but human nature as a whole. Jesus, the evangelist affirms, was both fully God and fully man.

The creed promulgated by the Council of Nicaea in 325AD is yet more explicit. It affirms belief in 'one Lord Jesus Christ, the Son of God, begotten from the Father, only-begotten, that is, from the substance of the Father, God from God, light from light, true God from true God, begotten not made, of one substance with the Father, through whom all things came into being, things in heaven and things on earth, who because of us men and because of our salvation came down and was made flesh and became man.'

Six preliminary points must be noted concerning this belief in Christ as God incarnate.

(a) As I observed towards the end of the previous chapter, the belief presupposes the concept of creation. Hence Athanasius affirmed the concept at the beginning of his *De Incarnatione*. Hence too the Nicene creed begins with a profession of belief in God as the Creator. In this century (as A. M. Ramsey has shown)[1] Gore's christological dispute with such Modernists as Rashdall and Major rested ultimately on the fact that whereas he interpreted the Incarnation in terms of the contrast between the Creator and the creature they interpreted it through the Hegelian view that all men are, in varying degrees, expressions of the Absolute.

(b) Because the Creator and his creatures are substantially distinct Godhead and manhood in Christ were, though inextricably united, unmixed. Therefore the Chalcedonian Definition (formulated in 451) affirms that in Christ the divine nature and a human nature co-existed 'without confusion' as well as 'without separation'. Similarly the so-called 'Athanasian' creed affirms that Jesus, as the God-man, 'is one, not by the transformation of the divinity into flesh, but by the taking up of his humanity into God.'

(c) Jesus was the incarnation of the Son or Word. According to the doctrine of the Trinity God exists as one 'substance' in the three 'persons' of the Father, the Son and the Holy Spirit. Although each person possesses the whole nature of the Godhead each is a distinct mode of being. And it was the Son, not the Father or the Spirit, who becomes man in Jesus.

(d) Jesus was God incarnate from the beginning of his life. This rules out adoptionism (the view that Jesus was originally only human and that he was 'adopted' by the Word and so made divine). Adoptionism is untenable on the following grounds. First, at what point in Christ's life is the act of adoption to be located? It cannot be later than the beginning of his public ministry. Was it at his baptism? Any answer we give to these questions is bound to be conjectural. Secondly, adoptionism involves an incredible dishotomy in the life of Jesus. A person's identity is constituted by his whole history from the moment of his conception to the moment of his death. Everything in his past contributes in some way to his present and his future. To postulate an adoptive union for Jesus is to postulate two wholly different lives for him - an ordinary human life up to the age of (say) twenty-eight and a life that was divine as well as human for (say) the two or three years between his baptism and his crucifixion. Thirdly, if Jesus was not divine from the beginning the Incarnation was incomplete. Lastly, adoptionism undermines the 'divine initiative' and thereby restricts the action of divine love. Alan Richardson puts this criticism thus. 'If God had to wait until a man good enough to be adopted as his Son happened to appear the central affirmation that God *sent* his Son into the world to redeem and save it would have to be abandoned. And then the love of God towards sinful men would become questionable. There is the world of difference between the view (which came naturally to the Greeks) that a man became God and the proclamation that God became man.'[2]

(e) Jesus was *fully* divine. This rules out subordinationism (that is, the view that Christ as the Son was inferior to the Father in status and being). Although this view of Christ was held by so great a theologian as Origen it is incompatible with belief in God's unity and infinity. At first sight it may seem to reconcile the affirmation of Christ's deity with monotheism in so far as it assigns supremacy to God the Father. Yet it inevitably leads to the postulation of two gods of whom the second is limited both *per se* and in the extent to which he merits our devotion. It is noteworthy that the author of the fourth gospel says at the beginning that the World was, not divine (*theios*), but God (*theos*). To say that the Word was divine could leave room for subordinationism which can be excluded only by affirming an identity of being between him and God. Of course the Son is subordinate to the Father in the sense that he is derived from the Father, but if (as the Nicene creed and Athanasius make plain) he receives the Father's whole nature, he and the Father are co-equal.

(f) The Incarnation is a *permanent* reality. When Jesus was exalted to 'the right hand of the Father' he did not discard his human nature. He retained it for ever, no longer in weakness and humiliation, but in a glory that is indestructible. The following reasons compel us to affirm the permanent continuation of his humanity in his exalted state. First, if his humanity could be separated from his deity he would have been a temporary theophany and not a full incarnation of God. Secondly, our whole redemption depends on the fact that the Christ who died and rose again in Palestine is present among believers here and now through the Holy Spirit. Thirdly, the New Testament claims that at 'the end' everything will be fulfilled in Christ.

This, then, is the essence of belief in the Incarnation. I shall now examine two basic objections to the belief.

First, it may be said that if the divine and human natures of Christ were distinct there was no real incarnation. However, if they were not distinct we must assume that in Christ God either turned himself into a man or mingled his divine nature with a human one. Both of these views are incompatible with belief in God's immutability. Both, too, present us with Christ as one who was neither fully God nor fully man. The hypostatic union - the unconfused union of the divine nature and a human nature within the person of the Word - was the nearest that even God could come to us without impairing the integrity of the natures. And it is nearer than any human person can come to another. Only God can take another, human, nature into union with his own; for only he is the creative archetype of all that is.

Furthermore, because Christ's manhood existed in, and only in, union with the divine Son it was the immediate object of divine action. Christ's divine nature did not merely co-exist with his human nature. The former energized the latter continuously. This glorification of Christ's humanity by God's presence is the secret of his person. It was (except for a brief moment at his Transfiguration) concealed in the days of his flesh; and it was revealed only in part by his resurrection. Christians will not know it directly until the life to come when they will see God in the exalted Christ 'face to face'. Yet although we cannot perceive it or, therefore, describe it we can say two things concerning its effects. First, it enabled Jesus to offer his life as a perfect embodiment of the dependence on and love for the Father that constitute the being of the Son within the life of the Trinity. Secondly, it enabled him to embody God's saving will. In both these ways it conferred on him a significance and a power that cannot be possessed by any other human being.

These observations lead to a major principle of christological language. From the beginning Christians have interpreted the Incarnation in terms of God becoming man. Thus the author of the fourth gospel says that 'the Word became flesh'. Yet more concretely the Nicene creed affirms that the Son 'came down' from heaven. It is inevitable that from our human standpoint we should speak of the Incarnation as a divine descent to our world. Thus even if we do not use the language of the Bible or the creeds we find it natural to speak of

God 'entering the sphere of our humanity' and 'subjecting himself to human conditions'. Yet the danger of such language is that we think of the Incarnation as an act whereby God compressed himself within the limits of a human life. The very idea of such a compression is absurd. The infinite cannot be contained within the finite.

In order to reach a final understanding of the Incarnation we must interpret it, not as a descent of God into a human nature, but as an act whereby God elevated a human nature into union with his own. E. L. Mascall states the truth thus (with special reference to kenoticism - that is, to the view that in order to become man God abandoned or suppressed all or some of his attributes). 'What, when expressed in the language of our experience is a making of God into flesh, is, when expressed from the divine standpoint, an exaltation of manhood into God. And it is God's standpoint, not ours, that expresses the ultimate truth.'[3] In this elevation (which of course must be understood in a purely spiritual sense) because the divine and human natures remained distinct and because a creature cannot add to or subtract from divine perfection God's nature remained unchanged. And unless it had remained unchanged Christ would not have been fully divine.[4]

The second objection to the doctrine of the Incarnation is that it is irrational. Here it is necessary to make a distinction between statements that are supra-rational (above reason) and those that are irrational (contrary to reason). The doctrine is, as theologians have continually admitted, supra-rational in the sense that the reality to which it points eludes our comprehension. We cannot understand how God became man. We cannot explain it through any concept drawn from our experience. This is inevitable. If God himself is incomprehensible his act in becoming man must also be so.

However, is the doctrine irrational? Is it self-contradictory? Undoubtedly it is paradoxical. Yet 'paradox' can have many meanings that are stated thus in the *Shorter Oxford English Dictionary:* 'seemingly absurd though perhaps really well-founded statement; self-contradictory, essentially absurd, statement; person, thing, conflicting with pre-conceived notions of what is reasonable or possible'.

The doctrine of the Incarnation is a paradox in the first and third of these senses. It certainly *seems* absurd to affirm that the same person is both God and man, both uncreated and created, both eternal and temporal. Also it conflicts with 'preconceived notions of what is reasonable or possible'. Hence it was a stumbling-block to the Jews and folly to the Greeks. Is it also paradoxical in the second sense? Is it *in fact* self-contradictory or absurd?

My answer to these questions will be based on two presuppositions. First, whether the doctrine is self-contradictory is a hard question to answer. Let us take, as a text-book illustration, the statement 'This table is both round and square'. Anyone can see that this is self-contradictory; for roundness and squareness are 'closed' concepts that are identifiable through sense-experience; so that we can see at once that they are mutually exclusive. But deity and humanity are 'open' concepts. They can be defined in various ways. And none of us is immediately acquainted with deity. Therefore the question whether they are incompatible cannot be settled without careful reflection.

Secondly, if a statement is self-contradictory it cannot be factually significant. If we say 'A cannot co-exist with B' we are not merely stating a linguistic convention or even a logical necessity. We are also stating a *factual* necessity - namely, that because A excludes B in the realm of thought it must also exclude B in the realm of extra-mental being. If we cannot conceive the co-existence of A and B they cannot co-exist.

Now, if we affirm that the divine and human natures in Christ were mixed so as to form a being who was half-God and half-man we are indeed affirming a contradiction. But if we affirm that the two natures were, though inseparable, unconfused the following factors, I maintain, are sufficient to rebut the charge that the doctrine of the Incarnation is self-contradictory.

(i) Manhood is not alien to Godhood. On the contrary the former is a created copy of the latter. Here we must remember the Biblical doctrine of the *imago Dei*. All creatures possess some degree of likeness to their Creator; but only man bears the Creator's 'image'. Only he is like God, not merely in this or that property, but in his essential nature. Thus while a lion resembles God in its strength a man resembles him in manhood (that is, in those spiritual properties that distinguish man from all other terrestrial creatures). Hence man is intrinsically adapted to any union with God that God chooses to confer.

(ii) Because a human person is made in God's image his nature is fulfilled to the extent that he confesses his dependence on God and seeks to obey God's will. The more dependent and obedient a person is the more truly human he becomes. No one could be as dependent on God as one who existed (as Jesus existed) solely through union with God. Correspondingly the obedience that the union necessitated meant that Christ's humanity exceeded, not fell short of, the humanity that in other men is scarred by sin.

(iii) There is at least one important example in the created order of two contrasting entities being brought together in such a way that the integrity of both is preserved. This is the union of soul and body (with which the Incarnation has often been compared). Furthermore, just as the Word governed his human nature without infringing it, so the soul governs the body. Admittedly some philosophers object to the view that mind and body are ontologically distinct on the ground that two such different principles of activity cannot co-exist in one entity. Yet if we have good reasons - and in my opinion the reasons are conclusive - for holding that mind is distinct from matter we must concede the fact of their co-existence although we cannot explain it. In the case of the human self we must posit a minor and partial mystery that prefigures, however faintly, the absolute mystery of the Incarnation.

(iv) The whole of evolution bears witness to the fact that lower forms of being are taken up into and enhanced by higher forms without losing their distinctive character. Thus the inorganic is included in the organic, and the organic in mental life. Through being thus included they acquire powers that they could not otherwise possess. At the same time they retain their own modes of being. Similarly in the Incarnation manhood is assumed and transformed by the Godhead without ceasing to be human.

Although these considerations do not explain the Incarnation in the sense of making it plain to human understanding they are sufficient to prevent us from ruling out the whole idea of a God-man as being self-contradictory or absurd. And that is all I claim for them.

I shall now indicate the New Testament's evidence for belief in the Incarnation. The New Testament undoubtedly presents Christ as one who was wholly human. The question is whether it presents him as one who was also divine. In examining this question it is necessary to distinguish between those passages in the New Testament in which belief in Christ's deity is explicitly affirmed and those in which it is implied. Of the passages in which it is explicitly affirmed the clearest instance is the Johannine prologue where Jesus is identified with the pre-existent Word who both was with God and was God. The prologue is corroborated by many statements later in the gospel. Among the sayings attributed to Jesus it is enough to cite Jn 8.58 ('Before Abraham was, I am'), Jn 10.30 ('I and the Father are one'), and Jn 17.5 ('Father, glorify thou me in thy own presence with the glory which I had with thee before the world was made'). Apart from Jesus's own words, the clearest evidence is the confession of Thomas in Jn 20.28 ('My Lord and my God'). The closest Pauline parallels to the Johannine prologue occur in the Epistle to the Colossians. In Col 1.19-20 Paul writes of Christ that 'in him all the fullness of God was pleased to dwell, and through him to reconcile to himself all things whether on earth or in heaven'. Later, in Col 2.9, he affirms that in Christ 'the whole fullness of deity dwells bodily'. To these texts I should add Philippians 2.6 which affirms that Christ pre-existed in the form (*morphe*) of God, and which the N.E.B. renders: 'For the divine nature was his from the first'.

It would be difficult, however, to justify the doctrine of the Incarnation from a Biblical standpoint solely on the score of these passages and a few others like them. The crucial question is whether these affirmations are grounded in the total apostolic experience of Christ. In other words do Acts and the epistles afford *implicit* testimony to Christ's deity? I suggest that they do so in the following ways.

1. There are many places in which Jesus is referred to simply as Lord (Kurios). This and Christ (Christos) are the most frequently used titles for him. The simple and basic point I immediately wish to make is that throughout the New Testament Jesus's lordship is never qualified.

Whenever he is called 'Lord' it implies that his rule is absolute and that he therefore merits absolute devotion. When we remember that according to Jewish monotheism absolute sovereignty belongs to God alone; that in the Septuagint Kurios was regularly used to translate the divine name; and that the New Testament writers apply to Jesus Old Testament texts in which 'Lord' refers to God the implications are obvious.

2. The New Testament accords to Jesus a worship that is due to God alone. Such worship is implied in the unconditional ascription of lordship to him. Also it is explicit in several places. The chief evidence is Philippians 2.10-11 where Paul, perhaps quoting from a hymn that already existed in the Church, writes: 'Therefore God has highly exalted him and bestowed on him the name which is above every name; that at the name of Jesus every knee should bow, in heaven and on earth and under the earth, and every tongue confess that Jesus Christ is Lord, to the glory of God the Father'. Here there is a reference to Isaiah 45.23 where Yahweh is regarded as the object of adoration. Revelation 5.12, with its adoration of the heavenly Christ, is probably yet more familiar; 'Worthy is the Lamb who was slain, to receive power and wealth and wisdom and might and honour and glory and blessing'.

3. At many points the phraseology of Acts and the epistles implies an equation of Christ with God. In the sermon recorded in Acts 2.14-36 Peter says of the risen Christ: 'Being therefore exalted at the right hand of God, and having received from the Father the promise of the Holy Spirit, he has poured out this which you see and hear'. In thus conveying the eschatological gift of the Spirit Jesus performed a task that the prophets inevitably reserved for God. Next let us consider the epistle to the Romans. In chapter 8 Paul speaks interchangeably of 'the Spirit of God' and 'the Spirit of Christ', 'the love of Christ' and 'the love of God' so that it is not surprising that in 10.13 he applies to Jesus words that in the Old Testament were applied to God. Again, in the benediction at the end of 2 Corinthians he associates 'the grace of the Lord Jesus Christ' with 'the love of God' and 'the fellowship of the Holy Spirit'. There are many other such triadic passages in the New Testament. I shall refer to them in the next chaper.

4. There is the exclusiveness that the apostolic writers assign to Christ as the agent of divine salvation. Thus according to Paul it is through Christ alone that we are reconciled to God; Christ alone is the expiation of our sins; he alone is the source of our sanctification. Christ supersedes all previous redemptive media, even those that were held as most sacred in the history of Israel. He is 'the power of God and the wisdom of God'. The question then is whether he could have been the all-sufficient mediator of God's wisdom and power unless he had, in his own person, possessed them. To say that one man is the total expression of God's saving will amounts to saying that he is one with that will in his inmost being.

5. There is the eschatological role assigned to Jesus. In the New

Testament he is represented as one who, by his death and resurrection, defeated the powers of evil and embodied, within this order of space and time, the eternal life of the age to come. Yet if he had been only a man could he have discharged this role? Surely a mere man, even if he enjoys perfect communion with God, can overcome evil only in his own life and to the extent that his own situation permits; he cannot overcome all evil and found a wholly new creation.

6. According to the New Testament the risen Christ actually communicates his life to believers. Christians 'dwell' in him as 'members' of his 'body'. Yet how could one finite person possess this power of self-communication? A saint can inspire others by his example; but he cannot impart to them the life that is his own. Thus even if we believe that St. Francis achieved spiritual perfection and now enjoys the beatific vision we should find it wholly incongruous to assert that we are 'in him' and that he is 'in us'.

I have been able to give only an outline of the New Testament's evidence for belief in Jesus as God incarnate. Yet this outline is enough to show that the belief was not an addition to the original Gospel but was implicit in the first Christians' response to Christ as their risen Lord. Here I agree wholly with the conclusions reached by C. F. D. Moule in his *The Origin of Christology.*[5] Moule begins by distinguishing between an 'evolutionary' and a 'developmental' view of New Testament christology. He sums up the first view (which he rejects) thus. 'The tendency which I am calling "evolutionary" and which I want to challenge, is the tendency to explain the change from (say) invoking Jesus as a revered Master to the acclamation of him as a divine Lord by the theory that, when the Christian movement spread beyond Palestinian soil, it began to come under the influence of non-Semitic Saviour-cults and to assimilate some of their ideas; and also by appeal to the effect of lapse of time, which may itself lead to the intensification of terms of adoration. It is like the so-called Euhemeristic theory of how Greek mythology found its gods'.[6] He then expresses the 'developmental' view as follows. 'By contrast, the tendency which I am advocating as closer to the evidence, and which I call "developmental", is to explain all the various estimates of Jesus reflected in the New Testament as, in essence, only attempts to describe what was already there from the beginning. They are not successive additions of something new, but only the drawing out and articulating of what is there. They represent various stages in the development of perception, but they do not represent the accretion of any alien factors that were not inherent from the beginning; they are analogous not so much to the emergence of a new species, as to the unfolding (if you like) of flower from bud and the growth of fruit from flower'.[7] On exegetical grounds that I find wholly convincing Moule proceeds to claim that 'among the earliest datable parts of the New Testament (the most widely acknowledged Pauline epistles) experiences of Christ are reflected which are unprecedented in pre-Christian religious experience and which it is difficult to explain as borrowing from the Gentile world and which indicate nothing short of divine status for him';[8] that in the New Testament 'Jesus is consistently presented as one with God in a way in which neither man nor angel is';[9] and that 'essentially these writers are affirming Christ to be *homoousios* with God'.[10]

How then did the apostolic church come to believe in Christ as a divine figure? It could not have reached the belief by an inference from the Scriptures (our Old Testament) or from any other Jewish writing; for these nowhere predict an Incarnation. The absolute distinction that orthodox Jews posited between the Creator and his creatures made it impossible for them to imagine that God could become man. Admittedly they speculated concerning the existence of divine, or at least supra-human, mediators (such as a Word or Wisdom) between God and the world; but they never thought of these mediators as being embodied in a man. There could not be any greater incongruity than that betwen Jewish descriptions of the divine Wisdom and a man crucified as a messianic pretender. It is also incredible that the first Christians should have ascribed divinity to Jesus in order to assimilate their belief in him to non-Jewish concepts of a 'divine man'. The incredibility is double. First, there is no parallel in non-Jewish sources to the doctrine of the Incarnation.[11] Secondly, it would have been impossible for a Jew like Paul to qualify Jewish monotheism in order to accommodate his belief in a merely human Jesus to a Hellenistic cult of a saviour-god.

It is clear that in the apostolic church belief in Christ's deity was based, not on any kind of inference, but on an experience of the divine power that he exerted. Here again I agree with Moule when he contends that the New Testament writers described Christ as God's agent in creation because 'they experienced Christ himself as in a dimension transcending the human and the temporal'.[12] This experience took the forms I have indicated. The dominant, decisive and all-inclusive form was the experience of the exalted Christ as one who merits worship and adoration. Worship was dominant because it is the ultimate form of religious experience in the Judaeo-Christian tradition; it was decisive because according to theism worship is due to God alone; and it was all-inclusive because each other form of experience is contained in it. The fact of all-inclusiveness needs stressing. The first Christians did not worship Jesus *in vacuo* and by an inexplicable abandonment of Jewish monotheism; they worshipped him as, and by implication because he was, the mediator of eternal life, the sole channel of divine salvation, the bearer of the Spirit, the embodiment of God's love, the Lord who claims absolute devotion. In the succeeding centuries the worship of Christ continued to be the chief factor determining the Church's ascription of deity to him.

So far I have confined myself to the basis of the doctrine of the Incarnation in the faith of the apostolic church. What basis, if any, does the doctrine have in the evangelists' record of Christ's earthly life?

Here we encounter a major difference between the fourth gospel and the synoptic gospels. According to the fourth gospel Jesus explicitly claimed to be divine; but according to the synoptic gospels he did not claim it. I have assumed, for the reasons that are usually given, that at this point the synoptic gospels are true to history and that the divine claims ascribed to Jesus in the fourth gospel represent an interpretation of him in the light of apostolic faith. This assumption cannot be proved beyond all possible doubt; and no one has a right to pass *a priori* judgments concerning Christ's consciousness of himself in relation to God. Nevertheless I consider the grounds for the assumption to be strong enough for the theologian to regard it as at least an hypothesis with which he must reckon. Of course even if Jesus did not verbally claim to be divine it does not follow that he was not aware of being so; but his words (as these are reported in the gospels) are the only evidence we have for his self-consciousness; and we have no warrant for inferring from his words modes of awareness that the words themselves do not express.

However, although the synoptic gospels do not say that Jesus claimed to be divine they offer many indications that he claimed to possess a unique status. Among these indications the following are the most impressive.

(i) Jesus affirmed that in his works the promised Kingdom of God had arrived. 'If it is by the finger of God that I cast out demons, then the Kingdom of God has come upon you.'[13] There are other texts in which Jesus makes a similar claim even when the word 'Kingdom' is not used. Thus through the images of the cloth and the wineskins he implies that he initiates a new order that supersedes the old.[14] Again, in a sermon preached in the synagogue at Nazareth he affirms that he has brought in 'the acceptable year of the Lord'.[15] So too in his reply to John the Baptist's disciples he makes is clear that he has instituted the new age of Isaianic prophecy so that he can say 'I tell you, among those born of women none is greater than John; yet he who is least in the Kingdom of God is greater than he'.[16] Jesus, then, proclaimed that in him the divine Reign predicted for the 'last days' had arrived and that therefore in him God's purpose for Israel was fulfilled.

(ii) There is the spiritual authority that Jesus claimed and conveyed. From the beginning of his ministry he impressed his listeners as one who taught with an authority not possessed by the scribes and Pharisees.[17] He continued to exhibit this authority in many ways - in his readiness to promulgate new commandments in his own name, in his assumption of a divine prerogative in forgiving sins, in his claim that salvation consists in obeying *his* words and following *his* example. He did not teach on the authority of Moses or, still less, Pharisaic tradition. He taught solely on the ground of his own insight into God's will and out of his immediate conviction that God's will was embodied in himself.

The substance of the preceding paragraphs is confirmed by the conclusion that W. D. Davies draws from his study of the Sermon on the Mount. 'Jesus passed beyond all principles he had inherited, beyond the light of Law and Prophet, to what we can only call an intuitive awareness of the will of God in its nakedness.'[18] A little later Davies adds these words. 'Whatever the actual teaching of Jesus about the future, the distinctive element in his teaching and activity was the realization that, in his ministry, the Kingdom of God was present. It is this that illumined him - his awareness of the Sovereign Rule of God in and through himself. This meant that whereas for Judaism the Law expressed the will of God, for Jesus his immediate awareness of the will of God became Law.'[19]

(iii) Jesus claimed a unique relation to God by addressing him simply as 'Father' (*Abba, Pater*). *Abba,* being the mode in which a son addressed his human father, was thought by the Jews to be too intimate a mode of addressing God. Hence Paul says that Christians can call God *Abba* because they are sons of God, not by nature, but by adoption and grace.[20] Jesus further affirmed that as the Son he is the sole means by which the Father can be known. 'No one knows the Father except the Son and anyone to whom the Son chooses to reveal him.'[21]

In all these ways Jesus is depicted as claiming a status higher than that claimed by any prophet or rabbi. The question that confronts us is whether this status is compatible with the view that he was merely human. Could a mere man validly claim to embody God's Reign, to exert unconditioned (even divine) authority and to be the sole means by which knowledge of the Father is obtained? And so (to say the least) the synoptic portrait of Jesus compels us to wonder. I mean both 'wonder at' and 'wonder whether' - wonder at the sheer fact of this extraordinary man and wonder whether he possessed a supra-human form of being.

Admittedly for those Christians who have assumed that the fourth gospel records the very words of Jesus it is disturbing to be told that he did not claim to be divine. Yet I suggest that the synoptic gospels' oblique way of witnessing to his deity is eminently congruous with a real incarnation. If he was both truly God and truly man it is appropriate that at every level of his earthly life his deity should have been simultaneously revealed by and concealed in his humanity. If he possessed both a divine nature and a human consciousness (as an element in a human nature) we can reasonably believe two things about him. On the one hand, being fully human he would not have been overtly aware of himself as one who in his pre-existent state shared his Father's glory and who incarnated it on earth. On the other hand, being fully divine he would have been conscious of enjoying an incomparably close relation of sonship to the Father; he would have been conscious too of embodying the Father's Kingdom (or Reign); and so he would have claimed an absolute authority not given to any other man.

Also according to the synoptic gospels Christ's disciples did not perceive his deity in the days of his flesh. Obviously if Christ himself was not explicitly aware of his deity his disciples could not have perceived it. But there are two further reasons for this lack of perception. First, the Jews did not expect an incarnation of God and so they were unprepared for the signs of it in Christ's earthly life. Secondly, God's revelation in Christ was not complete until the Resurrection and Pentecost. Hence it was only after these two events that his divine status could be grasped. This is clearly shown by the christological sequence of the New Testament. Thus even if Peter confessed Jesus as the Messiah at Caesarea Philippi he did not apprehend him as the divine Lord until he had risen and the Spirit had been given.

It therefore follows from the nature of Christian revelation that the primary evidence for the doctrine of the Incarnation should be the faith of the apostolic church. To say this is not to disparage the evidence provided by the gospels that are christologically indispensable on many grounds. Without them we should not have any means of identifying the risen Lord in whom the apostolic church believed. Without them, moreover, we should not have any means of knowing that the claims made for Christ by the apostolic writers were justified by the quality of his life. In any case the life of the human Jesus is itself revelatory in various ways of which I have stated only some. It would be fatally inconsistent to exalt the last stages in the sequence of divine revelation at the cost of underestimating the first.

I shall now examine the ways in which the early Church formulated the doctrine of the Incarnation. Here the two main landmarks are the council of Nicaea in 325 and the council of Chalcedon in 451. Throughout the centuries christology has been determined, directly or indirectly, by the formulae that these two councils produced. Hence a consideration of the Nicene creed and the Chalcedonian Definition is inevitable.

The Council of Nicaea was prompted by Arius and his disciples who held that Christ was a creature (*ktisma, poiema*); that he was brought into being at a particular moment in time; that his knowledge of the Father was imperfect; and that he was liable to change and sin. Of these tenets the most important is the first - the assertion that Christ is merely a creature (albeit the most perfect among creatures in so far as, according to Arius, he was produced before all others and was the instrument through which they were created). In reply the Nicene Creed affirmed beyond doubt belief in Christ's deity. 'We believe', it runs, 'in one Lord Jesus Christ, the Son of God, begotten (*gennethenta*) from the Father, only-begotten (*monogene*), that is, from the substance (*ousias*) of the Father, God from God, light from light, true God from true God, begotten not made (*gennethenta ou poiethenta*), of one substance (*homoousion*) with the Father, through whom all things came into being'.

Some comments are required on the words *ousia* and *homoousion*.

Although *ousia* is often translated 'substance' its basic sense is 'being'. Here we need consider only two meanings that it could have. These correspond to the distinction that Aristotle made in his *Categories* between primary and secondary substance (*prote* and *deuterǫ ousia*). First, *ousia* could mean a single, individual, entity. This is Aristotle's 'primary substance'. Thus the *ousia* of Peter signifies Peter himself as an individual member of the human species. Secondly, *ousia* could mean the nature that entities have in common. This is Aristotle's 'secondary substance'. Thus the *ousia* of Peter signifies the human nature that he shares with other persons. In the creed the first sense is ultimately required. If Christ is divine and God is indivisible they must constitute one entity. However, two facts make it probable that the Nicene Fathers intended only the second sense. First, this was the sense that *ousia* normally had in the ante-Nicene Fathers. Secondly, the question that faced the council was whether Christ shared God's nature.

After Nicaea, then, there was no doubt in orthodox circles that Christ was divine. The next question to be determined was the way in which his deity was related to his humanity. Here the main dispute lay between Nestorius, bishop of Constantinople, and Cyril, bishop of Alexandria. Both believed in a real union of Godhood and manhood in Christ; but they expressed the belief differently. Nestorius held that the two natures were joined by a perfect 'conjunction' (*synapheia*) through which they were made one 'person' (*prosopon*). To Cyril this language seemed insufficient. He substituted for the idea of 'conjunction' the idea of union (*henosis*), and for the term *prosopon* the term *hypostasis*. In itself the change from *prosopon* to *hypostasis* was unimportant, for both words could signify a unitary being or individual reality. The important fact is that Cyril equated *hypostasis* with the Word, the second member of the Trinity. In his view it was the Word, *qua* an *hypostasis* of the Godhead (an individual form of the one divine Being) who constituted Christ as a single entity. (By Cyril's time *hypostasis* was commonly used to signify a person of the Trinity.)

Although Cyril may have misunderstood Nestorius at some points, the latter's christology (even when it is most favourably presented) has two grave defects. First, in speaking of Christ's divine and human natures being linked by 'conjunction' and 'indwelling', Nestorius failed to demonstrate the absolute uniqueness of the Incarnation; for all true Christians are to some extent joined to God and indwelt by his Spirit. Secondly, he failed to show how the two natures became one entity. Cyril made the ground of union clear. The natures became one, he affirmed, through the action of the Word in uniting a human nature to his own. And so Cyril remedied the first defect in Nestorianism by showing how God's relation to Christ differed from his relation to all other men.

Cyril's Christology was vindicated at the Council of Chalcedon. This council first ratified the creeds promulgated at Nicaea and Constantinople, together with Cyril's epistles and Leo's *Tome*. It then produced the following Definition:

> Therefore, following the holy Fathers, we all with one accord teach men to acknowledge one and the same Son, our Lord Jesus Christ, at once complete in Godhead and complete in manhood, truly God and truly man, consisting also of a reasonable soul and body; of one substance with the Father as regards his Godhead, and at the same time of one substance with us as regards his manhood; like us in all respect, apart from sin; as regards his Godhead, begotten of the Father before the ages, but yet as regards his manhood begotten, for us men and for our salvation, of Mary the Virgin, the God-bearer; one and the same Christ, Son, Lord, Only-begotten, recognized in two natures, without confusion, without change, without division, without separation; the distinction of natures being in no way annulled by the union, but rather the characteristics of each nature being preserved and coming together to form one person and subsistence, not as parted or separated into two persons, but one and the same Son and Only-begotten God the Word, Lord Jesus Christ.

This succinct and carefully worded Definition achieved three aims. First, it laid equal stress on the full deity and the full humanity of Christ. Secondly, it affirmed both the distinctness and the inseparability of the two natures. Lastly, it affirmed their unity within one 'person' (*prosopon*) and 'subsistence' (*hypostasis*). Two points must be noted concerning this Definition.

First, the word translated 'person' is used in an ontological, not a psychological, sense. No single word suffices as a translation of it and of its equivalent, *hypostasis;* but 'individual being' or 'concrete reality' will serve as paraphrases. Christ's divine and human natures constitute one individual being or concrete reality. The negatively important point to note is that 'person' does not mean 'personality' in our modern, psychological, sense of a self-conscious ego possessing spiritual qualities. The Chalcedonian Fathers did not, and perhaps could not, explicitly consider the concept of personality in this sense. Yet if they had done so they would certainly have said that because God is personal and because Christ was fully human Christ possessed two personalities - the personality of the uncreated God and the created personality that God assumed. They implicitly affirmed that Christ possessed a human personality when they said that he possessed a 'rational soul'.

Secondly, although the Chalcedonian Fathers do not explicitly affirm how the divine and human natures of Christ are united to form one *hypostasis* they imply in two ways that the union occurs within the Word as the second person (*hypostasis*) of the Trinity. They endorse Cyril's epistles where this union is unambiguously affirmed. Furthermore, they speak of 'one and the same Christ, Son, Lord, only-begotten' and, still more emphatically, of 'one and the same Son and only-begotten God'. According to the Definition, then, it is the person of the Word who makes of his own nature and the human nature he assumed one, indivisible, reality. This interpretation of the Definition is supported by patristic scholars of unquestioned authority. Thus Grillmeier writes that 'Chalcedon leaves no doubt that the one Logos is the subject of both the human and the divine predicates' and that 'in the view of Chalcedon, Christ is not just a *"homo deifer"* or a human subject, *habens deitatem,* but the God-Logos, *habens humanitatem,* or rather, *habens et deitatem et humanitatem'.*[22]

This interpretation, too, is theologically inevitable. If we merely affirm that the two natures are one we fail to show the ground of their unity; and so we make the Incarnation unintelligible. It is clear that the ground of unity must consist in either the humanity or the deity of Christ. It cannot consists in the humanity; for no human being has the power to unite himself hypostatically with God; and in any case the idea of such a union would be exposed to the objections I have brought against adoptionism. This union must therefore be constituted by God. And since it was the Son, not the Father or the Spirit, who became incarnate it must be constituted by the Son as the second person (*hypostasis*) of the Trinity.

Nicene and Chalcedonian christology has often been criticized. I shall consider five main criticisms. Of these the first, second and third apply specifically to the Chalcedonian Definition. The fourth and fifth apply to the Nicene creed also. I shall maintain that all the criticisms are invalid and that assent to the substance, though not necessarily the wording, of the Definition is indispensable for elucidating the doctrine of the Incarnation.

1. It is sometimes said that the postulation of two natures in Christ is self-contradictory. This criticism would apply to any statement of the belief that Jesus was both God and man. And I have already given reasons for holding that this belief is, though a paradox, not a self-contradiction.

2. It is also sometimes said that the Chalcedonian Definition does not explain *how* the two natures are one. 'How' can have two meanings. It can mean a demand for the cause or ground of the hypostatic union. The Definition answers this question by implicitly affirming that the union is created by the *hypostasis* of the Word. 'How' can also mean a demand for some further insight into the mode of the hypostatic union. No such insight is possible. This union in itself is bound to be (as the Fathers constantly affirmed) a mystery. If we cannot comprehend God's self-existence and creativity we obviously cannot comprehend his supernatural act in becoming man. All attempts at explaining the inner nature of the hypostatic union are doomed to failure. The most conspicuous example of such attempts is the concept of *kenosis* (according to which God abandoned or suppressed some or all of his attributes in becoming man). The basic objection to this concept (apart from the particular objections that have so often been raised) is that it represents a futile effort to comprehend God's inner act at the moment of incarnation. This question of the Incarnation's incomprehensibility comes to a head when we interpret the Definition's ascription of two

natures to Christ in terms of self-consciousness. There are three modes of self-consciousness with which we must here reckon: God's self-consciousness within his own triune being (which I shall discuss in the next chapter), his consciousness of himself in his incarnate state, and the consciousness that the incarnate Son had of himself in his relation to the Father. What, then, was the relation between these three modes of self-consciousness? We cannot even begin to answer this question; for any answer would imply that we could imaginatively enter into the mind of God.

3. The Chalcedonian Definition is also sometimes attacked on the ground that it leaves the two natures juxtaposed, without any relation to each other. This is an unfair use of the *argumentum ex silentio*. The Chalcedonian Fathers were not required to pronounce on the relation between the natures. However, if they had been asked they would certainly have said that the natures were interrelated in the closest possible ways, and in particular that Christ's human nature was continuously activated by his divine nature. Thus Cyril wrote that 'we must therefore confess that the Word has imparted the glory of the divine operation to his own flesh'.[23] Even Leo, who distinguishes sharply between the two natures, affirms in his *Tome* that 'each nature performs what is proper to itself in communion with the other'. (*Agit enim utraque forma cum alterius communione quod proprium est*).

4. The christological language of the Nicene creed and of the Chalcedonian Definition - and indeed the language of the Fathers as a whole - has often been criticized on the ground that it distorts the Gospel by departing from the language of the New Testament in two respects.

(i) Whereas the New Testament describes God's relation to Christ in terms that are personal and dynamic the Fathers describe it in terms that are impersonal and static. The term 'substance' is often singled out for criticism on this score. Admittedly in modern English the word can suggest something that is impersonal or inert. But it must be noted that 'substance' is a translation via the Latin *substantia* of the Greek *ousia;* that *ousia* means, both etymologically and (in its most general sense) philosophically, 'being'; and that being can be of either a personal or an impersonal kind. So far as the contrast between the active and the static is concerned it is worth noting that Aristotle (whose indirect influence on Christian theology is often here unjustly deplored) systematically associated the concept of substance or being (*ousia*) with the concept of activity (*energeia*). In any case there can be no doubt that when the Nicene Fathers said that Christ was of one substance with the Father they meant by 'Father' the Creator whose personal and active nature was revealed in those redemptive acts to which the Bible testifies.

(ii) A further, more profound, objection is that whereas the New Testament describes Christ in terms of function and activity the Nicene creed and the Chalcedonian Definition describe him in terms of nature and being. I maintain that these contrasts, if pressed to the point of mutual exclusion, are false both historically and metaphysically. Admittedly the first Christians came to perceive a divine significance in Christ through their experience of his function in mediating God's redemptive activity. They apprehended his person through his work. Admittedly too the writers of the New Testament do not apply the words 'nature' (*physis*) or 'being' (*ousia*) to Jesus. Nevertheless they ascribe to him titles (such as 'Christ' and 'Lord') that are meant to indicate his personal status. Moreover Paul and John in effect affirm that Christ possesses God's nature by saying that he embodies the divine pleroma and incarnated the divine Word. In any case 'function' and 'activity' imply 'nature' and 'being'. Thus a wheel can function as a means of propelling a vehicle only if it possesses the properties of a wheel; and the sum of these properties taken together with their interrelation form the nature of a wheel. The same implication characterizes 'activity'. An activity is always of a certain kind. Thus a plant exhibits one kind of activity and a dog another. The similarities and differences between the kinds form the basis of classification. Yet to say that an activity is of a certain kind amounts to saying that it is of a certain nature. The nature of an activity is simply the set of characteristics that makes it this kind, in contrast with other kinds, of activity. Similarly 'activity' implies 'being', in the senses of both 'essence' (or 'nature') and 'existence'.

Yet my chief point is that the terms 'function' and 'activity' are either totally or partially inadequate as ways of stating the doctrine of the Incarnation. They are totally so if they are applied either only to God or only to Christ's humanity. Thus if we say merely that the human Jesus exercised a unique function as the mediator of divine salvation we make him out to be no more than the supreme example of those human persons who have revealed and performed God's saving will. Conversely if we say merely that God acted redemptively through Jesus we make out Jesus to be no more than the supreme example of those persons through whom God has thus acted. However, if we apply the terms both to God and to Christ's humanity we can partially affirm the Incarnation. Here is an instance of what I mean from James P. Mackey's *Jesus The Man and the Myth*.[24] 'To say that there are two natures, divine and human, in Jesus is simply tantamount to saying, what the followers of Jesus realized they must say, that Jesus functions as man and as God, since in Jesus they encounter one like themselves in all things, except that he was no sinner, and they encounter the one, true, God.' This formulation is successful in affirming the absolute uniqueness of Jesus as God incarnate; for we cannot say of any other man that he functions as God. The failure in the formulation is double. It does not affirm the fact or, therefore, the ground of the union between Godhood and manhood in Jesus; but both are affirmed by the Chalcedonian Definition. Moreover, in saying that Jesus functions as God and as man Mackey implies that there is a divine and a human nature that the functions express.[25]

5. Another, general, objection to the Nicene creed and the

Chalcedonian Definition is that they adopt a 'christology from above' (that is, a christology starting from the divine Son) instead of a 'christology from below' (that is, a christology starting from the human Jesus). We must here distinguish between the order of being and the order of knowing. Within the order of being the Incarnation is by its very nature 'from above'; it consists in an absolutely unique act whereby the eternal Son united a human nature with his own. Within the order of knowing belief in the Incarnation both must be and can be 'from below'. It must be so in so far as we know Christ's deity only through his humanity. It can be so in so far as it is possible for someone to begin by believing in Jesus as merely a man and then to apprehend him as also divine. Yet even within the order of knowing a 'christology from above' finally takes precedence in so far as we can finally understand Jesus and his humanly perfect response to God only in terms of God's prior act in becoming man for our sake. All knowledge is incomplete until it reaches a full correspondence of the mind with the object known.

If, for strictly theological purposes and with a view to christological description, we start with the human Jesus and then relate him to God two results are bound to follow. First, we shall make out Jesus to be different in degree, not in kind, from other men; and so we shall fail to state his absolute uniqueness as the incarnate Son. Secondly, although we shall state the effects of the Incarnation we shall not state the fact of it. Certainly Jesus was a man who was perfectly related to God in so far as he was wholly possessed by the Holy Spirit, wholly responsive to divine grace, wholly united to God by obedience and love. Yet these modes of relation do not state the absolute uniqueness of the Incarnation; for other men have exhibited them to lesser degrees. They state, not the divine fact of the Incarnation, but its human effects.

This is such an important matter, especially in terms of recent christology, that I shall illustrate it from three examples from writings produced by British theologians since World War 2. My first example is D. M. Baillie's *God Was In Christ.*[26] Baillie attempts to describe the Incarnation through what he calls 'the paradox of grace'. By this he means that in the Christian life all moral good is due simultaneously both to a man's free will and to God's grace. This paradox was perfectly exemplified by Christ. Thus Baillie writes: 'is it not the same type of paradox taken at the absolute degree, that covers the whole ground of the life of Christ, of which we say that it was the life of a man and yet also, in a deeper and prior sense, the very life of God incarnate?'[27] Yet on this view (as the quotation shows) Christ would differ in degree, but not in kind, from other men. Baillie is aware of this objection. He quotes Newman for claiming that 'God's presence and his very self, and essence all divine' is 'a higher gift than grace'. He also quotes Aquinas's distinction between *'gratia habitualis,* given to Christ, as man, like other men, and *gratia unionis,* given only to Christ'. But he strangely dismisses this as an 'artificial distinction'.[28]

Secondly, there is the essay that G. W. H. Lampe contributed to the symposium entitled *Christ, Faith and History*.[29] Lampe proposes that instead of interpreting the Incarnation in terms of an assumption of human nature by the Word we should interpret it in terms of the human Jesus's perfect possession by the Holy Spirit. 'By the mutual interaction of the Spirit's influence and the free response of the human spirit such a unity of will and operation was established that in all his actions the human Jesus acted divinely'.[30] However this view also represents Christ as one who differed in degree, but not in kind, from other men; for all prophets and saints are to some degree possessed by the Holy Spirit. Lampe himself admits that one reason why the ancient Church adopted a Logos-Son christology was that an interpretation of Christ in terms of Spirit-possession would not in itself secure belief in his absolute uniqueness as God incarnate. 'Orthodox belief was deeply suspicious of any theory which might seem to imply that Jesus was a "mere" man. To describe his relationship to God as an indwelling by the Spirit suggested that he was a prophet: greater, no doubt, than all other prophets but nevertheless, like them, an inspired man.'[31] Both Baillie and Lampe state two effects of the Incarnation in terms of the human Jesus's perfect response to God's grace and his perfect possession by the Holy Spirit; but they do not state the fact of the Incarnation or, therefore, Jesus's qualitative difference from other men. This fact and this difference consist, not in the human Jesus's relation to God, but in God's assumption of a human nature into union with his own.

The third theologian I have chosen is W. R. Matthews whose Maurice lectures entitled *The Problem of Christ in the Twentieth Century*[32] differ from the writings I have mentioned in their full recognition of the necessity of distinguishing between the fact and the effects of the Incarnation in order to secure belief in the latter's absolute uniqueness. On the one hand Matthews suggests that we interpret the Incarnation through the concepts of 'pattern' and 'inspiration'. Jesus was a man whose will exhibited an identity of pattern with God's will, and who was continuously inspired by the Spirit. On the other hand Matthews admits that these concepts must be supplemented by metaphysical (and specifically patristic) categories for the purpose of affirming the Incarnation *per se*. Thus on 'pattern' he writes that 'even if we were satisfied that, in one instance, a personal life showed the pattern of the divine will, we should still have to ask why, in this case alone, the pattern was perfect'.[33] He then claims that, from the standpoint of Christian faith, we can answer the question only if we affirm, with the Fathers, that the Incarnation was constituted by 'the taking of a created subject by the divine Logos and the intimate union with it so that the human subject, while never ceasing to be human and created, was so intimately joined with the divine that they formed, in the sphere of history, one person'.[34] Similarly he admits that the concept of inspiration refers, not to 'the ultimate and eternal ground' of the Incarnation, but to 'the person of Christ as a phenomenon in the order of history'.[35] In other words the concept signifies, not the divine fact of the Incarnation, but one of its human effects.

There is, however, one qualification that is required. It must be admitted that sometimes the Fathers were so anxious to affirm the deity of Christ that they tended to obscure belief in his full, concrete humanity. Yet this criticism cannot be brought against the Chalcedonian Definition that lays equal stress on both the deity and the humanity of Christ. In order to clarify this point I shall consider the concept of *anhypostasia* and relate it to the Definition. According to this concept Christ's humanity was impersonal or nonpersonal; he lacked a human person or hypostasis. The concept seems to me to be both true and false according to different senses that can be attached to 'person'. If by 'person' we mean an individuated form of human nature inhering in a subject-self or ego we must affirm that if Jesus was fully human he must have been thus personal. The Definition attributes personality, in this sense of the word, to him by saying that he possessed a rational soul and was consubstantial with us. Yet if we mean by 'person' an 'independent form of being' we must affirm (as the Definition implies) that Christ's humanity was non-personal in so far as, unlike the humanity of all other men, it existed only in union with the Word. Conversely we must in this sense endorse the concept of *enhypostasia.* Christ existed as a human being only 'in' the second person of the Trinity. If this had not been so he would not have been God himself living a human life for our salvation.[36]

I therefore conclude that the Chalcedonian Definition survives criticism and, moreover, that it is christologically indispensable in so far as it affirms that the person of Christ was constituted by the union of complete Godhood with complete manhood in the person of the Son. Two further points concerning the Definition and the Nicene creed need to be made. First, their authors do not interpret their terms through any one system of philosophy or theology. They leave the terms undefined and use them in the simplest possible manner solely in order to make explicit what was implicit in their total response to Christ as the divine redeemer. Secondly, their terminology is easily comprehensible. 'Nature' and 'being' are terms of universal application and are still constantly used by people who are neither philosophers nor theologians. And they are thus used with reference to both God and man. Admittedly *hypostasis* is a quasi-technical term that is bound to seem unfamiliar to someone who, without any prior knowledge of Greek, encounters it for the first time. Yet even it becomes intelligible by the use of either 'person' (which the Definition gives as its equivalent) or one among the paraphrases I have offered. In both these respects these documents have a timeless quality that supports the authority that has been accorded to them by the Church.

I shall now consider two further questions that the doctrine of the Incarnation raises. The first of these concerns the relation between the

Incarnation and miracles. In the preceding chapter I defined a miracle as 'an unusual event of a physical or material kind that supersedes the laws of nature and is due to a supernatural act of God'. According to this definition there are three forms of the miraculous that are relevant to the Incarnation. These are the Virgin Birth of Christ, the miracles that Christ performed during his earthly life and the Resurrection. My question is this. Is belief in these miracles required by belief in the Incarnation? I do not think there is any theological requirement that would make it internally inconsistent for someone to believe in the Incarnation but not to believe that these miracles occurred. In other words we cannot validly affirm that if Christ was God incarnate he *must* have been virginally conceived, that he *must* have performed miracles, that he *must* have risen bodily. We cannot validly make these affirmations because we cannot obtain *a priori* insight into the scope and limits of God's action on and within the humanity he assumed.

However, we can see *a posteriori,* in the light of Christian revelation as a whole, that these miracles are appropriate to the Incarnation. The virginal conception of Jesus was an appropriate way of signifying the fact that his birth marked the beginning of a new creation. If Christ performed miracles his performance of them, as signs of the Kingdom's advent, would have been wholly congruous with the fact that his divine nature constantly energized his human nature and imparted to it powers that it could not otherwise possess. The crucial case is the Resurrection. It is reasonable to suppose that one effect of Christ's divine nature on his human nature would have been to prevent his body from disintegrating and to transform it into a new body of the kind that the evangelists describe. Moreover a bodily resurrection would uniquely signify, in a manner especially compelling for Jewish Christians, the fact that Jesus embodied within 'this age' the eternal life of 'the age to come'. It has been objected that if Christ rose bodily he was to that extent unlike us whose bodies decompose after death. Yet if Christ was God incarnate we must be prepared to find that his humanity was unlike as well as like ours. Apart from the Resurrection his humanity, according to the New Testament and the Fathers, was unlike ours is being sinless. Futhermore, we must remember that Christ's death was fully real; that in dying he came to terms both with his death and with the factors that caused it; and that by the manner in which he came to terms with them he accomplished our salvation.

Yet it is important to distinguish between the miraculous and the supernatural, and to give theological priority to the latter. In a theistic context 'supernatural' can have either a general or a particular reference. It can refer, generally, to God himself as the transcendent Creator. Or it can refer specifically to those actions of God that exceed his normal operations and that confer on the created order new powers that it cannot by its own nature acquire. I am now concerned only with the second reference. My initial point is that the miraculous and the supernatural are distinct notions, and that although the first implies the second the second does not imply the first. There are two forms of divine activity that are supernatural without being miraculous. These are the Incarnation and the new life that God imparts to believers through their union with Christ as their incarnate Lord. The Incarnation is obviously supernatural. The hypostatic union exceeds any relation between God and man that is possible simply through the actualization of the nature with which God endowed man by his act of creation. Similarly Christians receive a new, supernatural, mode of being through participation in the divinized humanity of the exalted Christ. Yet neither the Incarnation nor the super-naturalization of the creature by the Spirit of Christ is a miracle. Neither necessarily involves a suspension of any physical law. Both have been associated with miracles; but neither is itself miraculous.

What is of primary importance for Christianity is that it is supernatural in these two respects. Whether it is also miraculous is a secondary matter. The test-case is, inevitably, the Resurrection. Let us suppose that Christ rose bodily from the dead. The mere fact that he appeared in his risen form to his disciples for a period of forty days would not have saving significance. This significance is imparted to the Resurrection by the prior fact that the one who rose was God incarnate and by the subsequent fact that Christ confers his risen life on his disciples.

My second question is whether belief in the Incarnation is essential to Christianity. I maintain that it is so on the following grounds.

1. The belief is firmly based on the New Testament and the teaching of the Church. The New Testament's testimony does not consist in a few texts of which the exegesis in precarious; it pervades the apostolic books and is exegetically unassailable. Admittedly the New Testament writers state the belief in implicit more often than explicit terms. Yet this is to be expected if Christ's deity was concealed in as well as revealed by his humanity, and if the Incarnation was an unpredicted event. Moreover the belief is fully supported by the testimony of the post-apostolic church. It was in order to exclude Arianism and affirm Christ's deity that the first ecumenical council at Nicaea promulgated a creed that was endorsed by later councils, and that has been continuously regarded as a norm of faith by Christians of various denominations.

2. Belief in the Incarnation has ceaselessly permeated the spiritual and liturgical tradition of the Church. This is so vast an area that I can give only a few examples from liturgy. First, there is the recitation of the Nicene creed at the central act of the Church's worship, the eucharist. Secondly there is the repeated use of a trinitarian formula in prayers and doxologies. Again there are many hymns that depend for their evocative power on belief in Christ as God's incarnate Son. If such liturgical elements were to disappear the impoverishment of both public worship and private devotion would be immeasurable.

3. Only the doctrine of the Incarnation can justify traditional belief in the absolute uniqueness of Christ and of Christianity as one among the

world's religions. Let us first consider the person of Christ himself. If he had been merely a man specially inspired by the Spirit he would have been only one, even if the greatest, in a line of prophets, saints and martyrs. Even if he had possessed the suprahuman (though purely created) status that Arius accorded to him he would have been comparable with the angels. However if he was God incarnate and if the Incarnation was unrepeatable he must have been absolutely unique. Similarly the only absolutely unique element in Christianity - the only thing that distinguishes it wholly from all other religions - is the belief that the Creator became man in one figure of history. This point has been well made thus by J. A. Baker:

> 'The one totally new thing which Christianity brought into the world was the belief, hammered out over the first four-and-a-half centuries of its existence, that in Jesus of Nazareth God had been living a genuine human life. Other religions had gods walk the earth incognito, or had proclaimed the divinization of some hero or sage. Christianity alone took a historical person and said, "Here in this human personality, with all the limitations and suffering of our human condition, was the eternal God, the Cause and Origin of all that is". As defined in all its classical rigour this is the unique feature of the Christian religion, its only valid claim to separate existence. A God of goodness, a Creator who cares, it shares with Judaism and philosophical theism. A man who truly reflects the nature of the divine is no new thing to the Hindu or the Baha'i. A divinely inspired prophet, even one miraculously born, is acceptable to Islam. The Spirit of God indwelling men and guiding and strengthening their lives is a religious commonplace. Divine food received in a sacramental meal is Zoroastrian; ritual washings and initiation rites are found universally. Islam holds fast to judgment, heaven and hell; Judaism to repentance, amendment, and God's merciful pardon. At every point accommodation is possible save at this one: this unique claim about Jesus, with its undergirding in the doctrine of the Holy, Blessed and Undivided Trinity. If this goes then the end of Christianity as an independent entity cannot be indefinitely delayed. No Incarnation, no Christianity.'[37]

4. There is the question of the finality, or ultimacy, of Jesus as the revealer of God. By 'finality' I mean two, closely interrelated, things. First, no one can surpass or even be an equal to Jesus in his capacity to reveal God and God's purpose for mankind. Secondly, Christ, in both his person and his work, did not merely indicate this purpose in a uniquely authoritative way; he actual embodied and fulfilled it. Yet can Christ's finality be substantiated if he was merely human? I do not think so. How can we be sure that God will not send another man who will be equally (perhaps better) equipped to reveal him? Again, does it make sense to say that a mere man, a merely individual member of the human race, can embody the end (*eschaton*) and goal (*telos*) of history? To me it makes no sense at all. I can make sense of it only on the assumption that the human Jesus was God incarnate and so possessed, by derivation, the universality that belongs to the omnipresent Creator.

It may be said that we need not make these claims for Christ's uniqueness and finality. Yet to abandon them would be to renounce traditional Christianity in two respects. First, the claims are inextricably embodied in the New Testament and the writings of the Fathers. Secondly, they have dominated the Church's whole sense of mission to the world.[38]

This, then, is the nature and these are the grounds for belief in Christ as God incarnate. There is only one thing I want to say in conclusion. I do not claim to have produced an intellectual 'proof' of the incarnation that will be universally compelling. It is impossible to demonstrate even God's bare existence from non-religious premises. Therefore it is impossible to demonstrate thus that he has supernaturally revealed himself. All knowledge of him must rest on experience. And the experiential knowledge of his presence in Christ cannot be obtained apart from the Holy Spirit who proceeds from Christ and testifies to him. 'No one', Paul writes, 'can say "Jesus is Lord" except by the Holy Spirit'. The totality of Christian revelation consists in the self-disclosure of the Father *in* the Son and *through* the Holy Spirit. The doctrine of the Incarnation thus leads to the doctrine of the Trinity.

[1] *From Gore to Temple* (London 1960, pp 66-76).

[2] In his article on 'Adoptionism' in *A Dictionary of Christian Theology* (London 1969).

[3] *Christ, the Christian and the Church* (London 1967, p 43).

[4] Certainly the Incarnation was an act of divine self-limitation in the sense that God restricted the effects of his divine attributes on his human nature so that the finite integrity of the latter might be preserved. However, this self-limitation did not involve any change in - any suppression of (still less abandonment of) - the attributes themselves. Similarly the concept of divine self-giving does not involve the postulation of any change in God. We can indeed affirm that God gave himself to us in Christ in so far as, first, he himself, in the person of the Son, was the ultimate subject of Christ's human life; and, secondly, he imparted to that life the life that is his own in a wholly unique mode that constituted both lives, one, indissoluble, entity. Yet he himself remained unchanged in the whole course of this self-impartation.

[5] Cambridge 1977.

[6] p 2.

[7] pp 2-3.

[8] p 6.

[9] p 106.

[10] *ibid.*

[11] Thus James D.G. Dunn concludes that 'we have found nothing in pre-Christian Judaism or the wider religious thought of the Hellenistic world which provides sufficient explanation of the origin of the doctrine of the Incarnation, no way of speaking about God, the gods, or intermediary beings which so far as we can tell would have given birth to this doctrine apart from Christianity' *(Christology in the Making,* London 1980, p 253).

[12] op. cit., p 138.

[13] Lk. 11. 20.

[14] Mk. 2. 21-2.

[15] Lk. 4. 16-23.

[16] Lk. 7. 28.

[17] Mk. 1. 22.

[18] *The Sermon on the Mount* (Cambridge 1966, p 148).

[19] *ibid.*

[20] Gal. 4. 4-6.

[21] Mt. 11. 27 (= Lk. 10. 22).

[22] *Christ in Christian Tradition* (London 1965, p 490).

[23] Quoted by J. N. D. Kelly, *Early Christian Doctrines* (London 1960, p 322).

[24] London 1979, p 243.

[25] From the standpoint of N.T. scholarship a mutually exclusive contrast between a functional and an ontic christology has been acutely criticized by R. H. Fuller in his *The Foundations of N.T. Christology* (London 1969).

[26] London 1968.

[27] p 129.

[28] pp 127-8.

[29] Ed. by S. W. Sykes and J. P. Clayton (Cambridge 1972).

[30] p 124.

[31] p 120.

[32] Oxford 1950.

[33] p 73.

[34] p 80.

[35] p 82.

[36] This is the meaning that *enhypostasia* came to have in the orthodox Calcedonianism of the Eastern Church. J. Pelikan has shown that according to Maximus and John of Damascus the term meant 'having its being in the hypostasis and not being real in and of itself' (Chicago 1977, p 88). However by saying that Christ possessed a rational soul and body the Chalcedonian Fathers clearly affirmed that his humanity was fully personal in the sense of being individual and concrete, not merely universal and abstract. Similar affirmations had already been made by Cyril and Leo. Thus Kelly writes that according to Cyril Christ's humanity was 'real and concrete' and that 'the modern allegation that he regarded it as a collection of purely abstract qualities conflicts with his express language' (op. cit., p 319). Similarly Grillmeier claims, in words that have a modern, specifically 'existentialist', ring that 'Leo's Christ stands as a man in free decision before God' (op. cit., p. 471).

[37] This quotation comes from a talk that John Baker (now Bishop of Salisbury) gave in 1974 at King's College, London.

[38] It is easy to evade this crucial question whether the doctrine of the Incarnation is essential to Christianity. There is a trace of such evasion in Hans Küng's widely read book *On Being a Christian*. In the fifteenth of the twenty propositions he adds to the abridged version entitled *The Christian Challenge* (London 1979) he says that 'the ecumenical basis of all Christian churches is the biblical profession of faith in Jesus as the Christ, as the criterion for man's relations with God and with his fellow men. This profession of faith must be freshly translated for each new age' (p 333). Taken in itself this could be compatible with the view that Jesus was merely a humanly perfect revealer of God. Yet Küng proceeds to affirm, in conformity to the Chalcedonian Definition, that Jesus was, not only 'truly man', but also 'truly God', so that 'nothing is to be deducted from the truth taught by the ancient christological councils, so far as this is really covered by the New Testament' (pp 334-5). Why, then, did Küng not include a simple affirmation of Christ's simultaneous Godhood and manhood within the 'ecumenical' proposition itself?

CHAPTER 3
THE TRIUNE GOD

All theists believe that there is only one God, the Creator of heaven and earth. But only Christians believe that the one God exists in the threefold form of Father, Son and Holy Spirit. In the previous chapter I examined belief in a divine Dyad - in God the Father and God the Son who became man in Christ. In this chapter I shall examine belief in a divine Triad - in a God who exists not only as Father and Son but also as Holy Spirit. I shall first consider the Biblical grounds for the belief and then discuss fundamental problems that it raises.

The doctrine of the Trinity is firmly grounded in the New Testament. I have already exhibited the grounds so far as the Father and the Son are concerned. The apostolic writers also express belief in the Spirit as a third member of the Godhead. Here, once again, I can give only an outline of the evidence which is twofold.

First, in several places the Holy Spirit is personified as the fount of divine activity among Christians. 'In Acts', Wainwright calculates, 'there are sixty-two references to the Spirit. In eighteeen of these the Spirit is described in terms which suggest that he is a person who speaks, forbids, thinks good, appoints, sends, bears witness, snatches, prevents, is deceived, tempted, and resisted.'[1] The clearest Pauline parallel is Romans 8. 26-7: 'Likewise the Spirit helps us in our weakness; for we do not know how to pray as we ought, but the Spirit intercedes for us with sighs too deep for words. And he who searches the hearts of men knows what is the mind of the Spirit, because the Spirit intercedes for the saints according to the will of God.' These personifications became finally articulate in the fourth gospel where the Spirit is described as the 'other' Paraclete whom the Father will give (or, alternatively, whom the Son will send from the Father), who will testify to the Son, and who will thus guide believers into all the truth.

Secondly, there are several triadic passages in which the Father, the Son, and the Spirit are simultaneously distinguished and united. Thus, according to Matthew 28. 19, the risen Jesus commands his apostles to baptize all nations 'in the name of the Father and of the Son and of the Holy Spirit'. Within the Pauline epistles the best known example is the benediction in 2 Corinthians 13. 14 ('The grace of the Lord Jesus Christ and the love of God and the fellowship of the Holy Spirit be with you all'). The following are some among many other instances. According to Acts 2. 33 Peter said, in his sermon on the day of Pentecost: 'Being therefore exalted at the right hand of the Father, and having received from the Father the promise of the Holy Spirit, he (sc. Jesus) has poured out this which you see and hear'. Again, the author of Ephesians writes of 'one body and one Spirit, just as you were called to the one hope that belongs to your call, one Lord, one faith, one baptism, one God and Father of us all' (4. 4-6). Similarly, 1 Peter is addressed to those who are 'chosen and destined by God the Father and sanctified by the Spirit for obedience to Jesus Christ' (1. 2).[2]

It is often asked whether according to the New Testament the Spirit is personal. All depends on the meaning we give to this adjective. If we take it to mean an individual form of divine being and activity (and so equivalent to the patristic usages of *persona* and *hypostasis*) the answer is that only some passages of the New Testament (such as those I have quoted) refer to the Spirit in personal terms. Often 'Spirit' signifies, according to Jewish usage, the spiritual nature of God considered as a unity. However, in order to provide a Biblical basis for the doctrine of the Trinity it is not necessary to prove that all references to the Spirit imply that he is a distinct *persona* of the Godhead, just as in order to provide a Biblical basis for the doctrine of the Incarnation it is not necessary to prove that all references to Jesus imply belief in his deity.

Sometimes those who ask whether the New Testament regards the Spirit as 'personal' are using the adjective in its modern sense, and their question can be amplified thus. Does the New Testament endow the Spirit with a mind and will analogous to the minds and wills that constitute human beings as persons, in contrast with animals or things? It certainly does so. Obviously when 'Spirit' means simply the spiritual nature of the one God we must interpret it in personal terms if God himself is, as the Bible throughout presupposes, personal. The texts I have quoted further show that when the Spirit is conceived as an individual entity - a *persona* or *hypostasis* - it is also conceived as personal. Indeed, it is by his personal operations that the Spirit's hypostatic character is revealed.

Admittedly the New Testament's teaching on the Spirit is less developed than its teaching on the Son. Thus it nowhere affirms the Spirit's co-eternity with the Father. Also it never implies that the Spirit is the object of worship. There are several reasons for these facts. The basic reason is that in the time-order of revelation the gift of the Spirit was subsequent to the life, death and resurrection of the Son. Furthermore, his role within the sphere of redemption is to witness, not to himself, but to Christ. He was sent solely for the purpose of mediating the life of Christ to believers. Hence at the beginning affirmations of his distinctive status as a member of the Godhead were less numerous than similar affirmations concerning the Son. Finally, in the first century Christ was, whereas the Spirit was not, the subject of theological controversy (which was an immediate cause of doctrinal development in the early church).

The remarkable thing is, not that the New Testament's teaching on the Spirit is less developed than its teaching on the Son, but that it reached the degree of hypostasization found in the passages I have cited; for the latter have no Jewish precedent. In the Old Testament 'spirit' (*ruach*) when applied to God signifies either his nature or his presence in the world. The first sense is exemplified in Isaiah 31. 3: 'The Egyptians are men, and not God; and their horses are flesh, and not spirit'. As F. Baumgartel puts it, ' "flesh" is earthly fragility and weakness - its bearer is "man"; "spirit" is absolute power and majesty - its bearer is God'.[3] The divine spirit is active in various ways - in creating the world, in inspiring prophecy, in directing the work of craftsmen. It will be present in a new and final mode in the age to come when it will descend on the Messiah and renew Israel. However, it is never envisaged as a distinct mode of divine being; it is not personified; it is simply 'God himself considered as acting, as creating, as vivifying'.[4] This fact is well illustrated by the parallelism in Psalm 139. 7: 'Whither shall I go from thy Spirit? Or whither shall I flee from thy presence?'

Why, then, was the Church not content with a divine dyad? Why did it proceed to speak of the Spirit as a third member of the Godhead? The answer lies in experience. Just as the early Christians were compelled, not by any argument or inference but by experience, to believe in Christ as the divine Lord, so they were compelled to believe in the Spirit as a power that, though wholly one with the Father and the Son, possesses its own form of being. This experience of the Spirit was obtained through many means. Romans 8. 26-27 suggests that Paul obtained it most vividly through prayer. The Paraclete-sayings affirm that the Spirit is known as Christ's 'other self' who befriends disciples, giving them increasing insight into Christ's relation with the Father, and, by his indwelling presence, produces a living image of that relation in their lives. Acts and the epistles show that the Spirit's hypostatic character was also revealed in *glossolalia,* in the conversion of unbelievers, in his sanctifying power, in spiritual gifts *(charismata),* and in his whole activity of uniting Christians within the one body of which Christ is the head.

I therefore agree with K. E. Kirk[5] when he maintained that the doctrine of the Trinity was generated by, and must be ultimately justified by, not philosophical or theological speculation, but spiritual experience. 'Whatever philosophical or historical grounds might have pointed to the doctrine of three persons within the one Godhead, they would have been insufficient to establish it in face of its inherently supra-rational character; only empirical grounds could make it certain. This implies that for the recognition of distinct hypostases within the Godhead there must be, on the part of man, a conviction that he also has, or is competent to have, "personal relations" with each of them.'[6] Kirk amplifies this as follows. 'If we could recognize three distinct activities of the Godhead towards ourselves, each sufficiently universal to be the expression of a whole personality summed up in one activity, and not a mere attribute, allowing room for other attributes alongside itself; and could recognize, moreover, that these activities, so far from being intermittent, transitory and successive, were contemporaneous and continuous we should have empirical support for belief in three persons in one Godhead, as distinct from a belief in three attributes or three aspects of the Godhead only.'[7]

Later in the same essay Kirk particularizes the relationship between believers and the divine persons. His view is that we are related to the Father as Lord, to the Son by 'communion', and to the Spirit by 'possession'. The New Testament gives qualified support to this view. The qualification is that we must not restrict any of these relations to one member of the Triad. According to the New Testament Christ as well as with the Father is Lord, believers have communion with the Spirit as well as with the Son, and they are indwelt by the Son as well as the Spirit. Nevertheless, the experience of being possessed by the Spirit in the various modes I have indicated was the special way in which his status as the third person of the Godhead was first made known.

This experience of possession implied a two-fold relation between the Spirit and the Son. On the one hand the Spirit was apprehended as being identical in nature with the Son. Hence Paul could call him the Spirit *of* the Son, and speak interchangeably of being indwelt by the Son and being indwelt by the Spirit. On the other hand the Spirit was apprehended as being distinct from the Son by whom he is sent and to whom he testifies. To be possessed by the Spirit meant to be aware of Christ as one who is wholly present in two different, yet constantly interacting, modes: as the risen Lord who is exalted to the right hand of the Father, and as a person who still lives on earth, empowering and illumining his disciples so that they may share his glory.

In the light of this survey I shall answer three questions.

First, can we consistently rest content with a divine Dyad - the Father and the Son to the exclusion of the Spirit? I do not think so for the following reasons.

(i) Belief in the divine Spirit as the third person of the Godhead, like belief in the divine Son as the second person, is firmly grounded in the New Testament. Moreover, within the New Testament the beliefs are closely linked in both form and content. With regard to their form they are identical in the following respects. Both are inexplicable in terms of Jewish and Greek thought; both are based on experience, not ratiocination; both are acquired through and verified by their spiritually transforming effects. In terms of content they are interrelated within a single pattern of revelation. Belief in the Spirit is not an isolated addition to belief in Christ and to the conviction that the scriptures were fulfilled in him. The Spirit is experienced as being sent by the Son for the purpose of testifying to him and conveying to disciples the new life of the promised 'age to come'.

(ii) Although it is impossible to prove the existence of the Trinity by *a priori* reasoning it is possible to exhibit *a posteriori* a necessary link between the Son and the Spirit within the order of revelation. Apostolic experience implies the following assertions. On the one hand the human Jesus now lives in heaven. On the other hand he still lives on earth and communicates his heavenly life to believers. This self-communication must be given its full strength. For the first Christians the experience of the risen Christ was much more than the force of a memory. It was much more even than something that could be described as a telepathic communication from another world. It was a consciousness of Christ as one who was as fully and distinctly present among them after his death as he was in the days of his flesh. How, then, are we to explain this continued presence? We cannot explain it by saying that the human Jesus *per se* is omnipresent. My reason for affirming this is that the human Jesus was not and is not, universally, Man, but 'a' man. Although his humanity is universifiable by virtue of its union with the Word it is not itself universal. In itself it is individual even in its exalted state. Hence if it is to be omnipresent it can be so only if it is re-presented by another who fully shares the Son's divine nature and so is co-equal with the Father and the Son as a person of the Trinity[8]

The necessity of unity and distinctness between the Spirit and the Son is also exhibited by the order of redemption. Our redemption depends on two facts: first, Christ's victory over sin and death in his own person, and secondly the communication of his victorious life to believers. It is essential to the salvific nature of the first fact that the exalted Christ should be wholly other than us as one on whose perfect sacrifice we depend. It is equally essential that he remains identical with the Jesus who lived and died in Palestine. Moreover, it is essential that this Jesus was 'consubstantial' with us in every respect (including the possession of incommunicable individuality). Hence there is need of a co-equal 'other' who will communicate his risen life to believers. (iii) The Spirit's co-equality with the Father and the Son was ultimately affirmed by authoritative declarations of the Church. Thus the Constantinopolitan creed that was approved by the Council of Chalcedon professes belief 'in the Holy Spirit, the Lord and the Life-giver, who proceeds from the Father, who with Father and Son is worshipped together and glorified together'. Even more explicitly the Athanasian creed speaks of the Spirit in exactly the same terms in which it speaks of the Father and the Son. Hence one cannot consistently invoke the Church's authority for belief in the second person of the Trinity if one does not also believe in the third.

There are, however, many reasons why to some people the Spirit seems less real and concrete than the Son. First, the very word 'Spirit' is apt to suggest something vague and unsubstantial. But to a Jewish Christian the Greek *pneuma* would suggest the Hebrew *ruach* - namely, the spiritual power and presence of God himself. This point is far from being a trivial one. In every sphere of knowledge the associations of words help to determine our understanding of the objects to which they refer. Secondly, whereas the Son is, the Spirit is not, identifiable by reference to a concrete figure of history in whom he became incarnate.

The most profound reason why to many people the third person of the Trinity seems less real than the second is that they tend to separate the Spirit from Christ and, therefore, to separate their experience of the

Spirit from their experience of Christ. Yet it is a theological, and moreover a religious, mistake of the first order to presuppose these forms of separation. The Spirit, though not simply identifiable with the Son, is inseparable from the Son in his nature, just as the Son is thus inseparable from the Father. Hence the Son and the Spirit are inseparable in their forms of operation. *Opera Trinitatis ad extra sunt indivisa.* Hence too the experience of the Spirit is inseparable from the experience of Christ. To experience the Spirit is to experience Christ as existing in two distinct but interrelated modes – both as one who now shares his Father's glory in heaven and as one who is present among believers here on earth.

My next question concerns the ontological status of the divine Triad. Here there are two main views: an 'essentialist' and an 'economic' one. According to the first God is in his essence, apart from the world, triune. According to the second God generates the Son and the Spirit solely for the purpose of creating and redeeming the world. (The Greek word *oikonomia* was used by the Fathers to signify God's plan for and governance of the world within the spheres of both creation and redemption). The economic interpretation of the Trinity in turn takes two main forms. According to the first the distinction between the Three, once it has arisen, is fully real. According to the second (known as 'modalism') the Three are not really distinct (as one human person is distinct from another). The Son and the Spirit are merely modes of revelation in which the one divine Person expresses himself.

I shall examine these two forms of economic trinitarianism with reference first to the Son and secondly to the Spirit. I suggest that both views are exposed to three objections, and that the second is further exposed to a fourth.

(a) Both are contrary to the New Testament and to the ultimate outcome of patristic theology. The fourth gospel affirms that the divine Word and Son who became man in Christ was distinct from the Father before the creation of the world. Later Origen stated that the Father begets the Son eternally. His view was endorsed by the Nicene Fathers in their anathematization of Arians who said of the son 'that there was when he was not'.

(b) According to both views Christ does not reveal God's inner nature; for he reveals God only in so far as he is the incarnate Son; but (if economic trinitarianism is true) God in his essence lies beyond the Father-Son relationship. Christ could then still validly have said 'You who have seen me have seen the Father'; but he could not have validly meant by this, without qualification, 'You who have seen me have seen God'. Therefore it would be necessary to proceed beyond Christ in order to have a complete conception of divine being. Christ would be only a stage, even if the penultimate stage, in theological understanding. Any view we might then hold concerning God's inner nature would be a matter of speculation or mystical experience. Is God in himself characterized by some kind of unity-in-diversity that falls short of his economic self-diversification as Father, Son and Holy Spirit? Or is he in himself a pure monad? Christian revelation cannot assist us in our answers to these questions; for it presents us only with divine triunity.

(c) Economic trinitarianism is incompatible with (i) monotheism, (ii) divine immutability and (iii) the integrity of divine personality. It is incompatible with (i) in so far as it posits the Son as a 'second' god who is inferior to the Father in two ways. First, he is not co-eternal with the Father. Secondly, and chiefly, God is complete in his divine perfection without the Son because he is thus complete without the world for the sake of which the Son was produced. Obviously economic trinitarianism is incompatible with (ii) in so far as it posits a radical change in God from what he is in himself to what he becomes for the purpose of creation and redemption. I use the word 'radical' advisedly; for he who was originally one becomes more than one. Economic trinitarianism is also (iii) incompatible with the integrity of God's personality. An element of structural identity is essential to the idea of personality. But such an identity cannot exist in a person who, though being one *per se,* becomes more than one in his self-manifestation.

(d) The distinctive objection to modalism is constituted by modalists' affirmation that the divine modes are only temporary. The idea that the Son will, or even can, be reabsorbed into the Godhead conflicts with the New Testament's claims for him as the one in whom history will be summed up. These claims, let us note, are not extrinsic additions to apostolic faith. They are necessitated by the experience of Christ as one who, while being distinct from the Father, mediates the fulness of the Father's wisdom, love and power.

All these objections can also be raised to some extent with regard to the Holy Spirit. Admittedly the New Testament does not affirm belief in the Spirit's co-eternity with the Father and the Son. Yet the belief was later affirmed by the councils of the Church. Also if the Spirit was produced by the Father only for the purpose of creation and/or redemption he would not be fully divine and so, in his economic role, would not reveal the ultimate reality of the Godhead. Finally, a modalistic interpretation of the Spirit would conflict with the New Testament's claim that he is Christ's representative in embodying the *eschaton* and so fulfilling God's purpose for mankind.

I therefore conclude that we cannot rest content with an economic Trinity. We must proceed to affirm that God is essentially Father, Son and Holy Spirit. Of course the essential Trinity is also an economic Trinity. The God who exists essentially in a triune form operates in this form for the purposes of creation and redemption. Moreover it is through, and only through, the Trinity's redemptive operations that we know God is his essential triunity. We know the eternal Father as the one to whom Jesus prayed as *Abba;* and we know the eternal Spirit as the one who communicates the life of Jesus and who thereby makes us 'adopted' sons of God. My only negative contention is that the Trinity is not merely economic. It is primarily essential. Its economic operations follow from and, in a spatio-temporal mode, reduplicate its essential nature within the hidden life of God.

Is, then, belief in an essential Trinity an inference from belief in an economic Trinity? It can be so. I myself have just suggested arguments in favour of an essentialist, as against a merely economic, interpretation of trinitarian language. However, belief in the essential Trinity need not be inferential. Thus the fourth evangelist did not base his belief in the Son's pre-existence on rational demonstration. He reached it intuitively through reflection on the Logos-concept in the light of Christian experience. Also most Christians throughout the ages have begun by accepting the doctrine of the Trinity 'on authority'; so that for them belief in an essential Trinity and belief in an economic one have co-existed *ab initio*. Their growing awareness of the triune God's self-revelation has always been governed by their conviction that he is, in his inner being, Father, Son, and Holy Spirit. Furthermore, even when the essential character of the Trinity is inferred the inference does no more than make explicit what we already know implicitly. When an astronomer infers from stars he sees the existence of a star he cannot see he is postulating the existence of an object that is wholly distinct from the objects of which he has experience. Yet there is only one Trinity. In inferring its essential nature from its economic manifestations we merely come to a full recognition of the God with whom we are already acquainted.

The third question is the most complex one. How are we to describe the essential Trinity? According to the formula that has become a norm of orthodoxy God exists as one substance (*substantia, ousia*) in three persons (*personae, hypostaseis*). I shall elucidate this formula in its Greek wording in order to form a link with the christological formulae I examined in chapter two. *Ousia* (as I said) signifies two things: nature and numerical identity. Just as to say (in the words of the Nicene creed) that Christ is 'of one substance with the Father' is to say that he shares the Father's nature and is numerically identical with him, so to say that the divine Three are one substance is to say that they have the same nature and constitute one, indivisible, Godhead. *Hypostasis* here (as in the Chalcedonian Definition) has an ontological, not a psychological, sense. No one word adequately translates it; but it can be paraphrased as 'individual form of being'. Its meaning is therefore akin to the meaning of *hypostasis* in the Chalcedonian Definition. Just as the divine Son and the human Jesus constitute one individual reality, so the Son, by whom the hypostatic union is effected, is as much an individual reality as the Father and the Spirit. Once again the important negative point to note is that *hypostasis* does not signify 'person' and 'personality' in the senses that these words have today.

The formula 'one substance in three persons' is meant simply to affirm the fact of God's triunity in a way that excludes on the one hand tritheism (the view that there are three gods) and on the other hand modalism (the view that the Three are no more than temporary manifestations of a divine monad). The formula does not state how the one is Three or how the Three are One. Of course it is not possible to explain the Trinity in the sense of making it plain to our understanding. If God, considered merely in his unity, is incomprehensible his triunity must also be so. Nevertheless the question remains whether it is possible to elucidate the formula without falsely claiming to unveil the mystery that it indicates.

One means of elucidation that has often been proposed is the way of analogy. Two main types of analogy have been offered: the psychological and the social type. According to the first (associated especially with Augustine) the Three are compared to various faculties of the human mind or soul. Thus, to take Augustine's culminating example, the memory, the understanding, and the will, though distinct activities, form one, indivisible, *psyche.* The social analogy can be traced back at least as far as Tertullian. According to it the Three are comparable to three human persons. It may best be illustrated by a father, mother and child who, while being three individuals, form one family. Although both types of analogy have their uses both can be misleading, even heretical, it over-pressed. The first type can suggest modalism; for mental faculties are not distinct individuals but merely modifications of a single mind. By contrast the second type suggests tritheism. These defects are inevitable. No theistic analogy adequately represents God. Each is (to use I. T. Ramsey's language) a 'model' that needs to be 'qualified' in various ways if it is to mediate a 'disclosure' of divine reality.

Leaving aside analogies can we conceptualize the difference between the Three while preserving belief in their unity? The answer given by many theologians from Augustine to Barth - an answer to which I subscribe - is that we can do so by affirming that they differ only in their interrelation. Each possesses the one, indivisible, nature of God. They are distinct only in the relation that they have to each other. Thus the Father is distinct from the Son only in so far as he begets the Son, and the Son is distinct from the Father only in so far as he is begotten by the Father. The Three subsist as individual forms of being. Their individuality infinitely surpasses any individuality to which a human being can lay claim. Yet it consists solely in their mutual relationship. The concept of 'subsistent relations' has been expressed thus by Barth. 'The relation in God in virtue of which he is three-in-one are thus his being Father *(paternitas)* in virtue of which God the Father is the Father of the Son, his being Son *(filiatio)* in virtue of which God the Son is the Son of the Father, and his being Spirit *(processio, spiratio passiva)* in virtue of which God is the Spirit of the Father and the Son.'[9]

There is, however, a difference between Western and Eastern theologians here. The Western view (which is the one I have presupposed) is that the divine persons differ *solely* in their mutual relations. The Eastern view has been stated thus by Vladimir Lossky. 'The relations only serve to *express* the hypostatic diversity of the Three; they are not the basis of it. It is the absolute diversity of the three hypostases which determines their differing relations to each other, not *vice versa.*'[10] My reason for preferring the Western view is simply that I cannot see how we can preserve belief in God's unity and simplicity if we postulate a ground of differentiation between the Three that is other than their interrelation. The only other ground is the individuation of a common species. The Three would then be three independendtly existing instances of Godhead (as Peter, James and John are three independently existing instances of manhood). Each of the Three would then be a 'first substance' (in the Aristotelian sense of the term); and so they would be three 'gods'. To say that there is a third ground of differentation that is wholly unknowable is (as Lossky admits) to opt for complete agnosticism and, moreover, to posit a fundamental antinomy between the divine persons and the divine essence.

Admittedly the concept of subsistent relations is (to use I. T. Ramsey's terminology again) 'logically odd'; for it has no instantiation in the created order. Yet trinitarianism is not especially vulnerable on this score. Theistic concepts, like theistic images, can never be given positive content in terms of finite existence. They all point to God as an absolute mystery of being. The two questions we must ask concerning any concept are: 'Is the postulation of it necessary?', and 'Is the concept free from self-contradiction?'. I have already answered the first question. With regard to the second it is necessary to make the distinction I have already made between a paradox and a self-contradiction (that is, between a statement that seems to be self-contradictory and one that actually is so). It is, of course, highly paradoxical to affirm that A's individuality is constituted by its relation to B and C; for such a mode of individuation does not occur in the world of finite being. Yet it is not self-contradictory. It does not involve a union of opposites that, by definition and throughout the whole range of their application, are mutually exclusive (as would be the case if we said that the Son is both a substance and not a substance, or both a relation and not a relation).

Furthermore, although the language of subsistent relations is non-Biblical its origins lie firmly in the New Testament. So far as the Father and the Son are concerned it is enough to appeal to the fourth gospel. There we learn, on the one hand, that the Father and the Son are one and, on the other hand, that they are united by a relation of love. Hence the only difference between them must consist in that relation. It is legitimate to infer that the same difference exists between the Spirit and the Son if (as the New Testament affirms) the Spirit is the Son's 'other self' who presents disciples with the Son to the Father.

From this analysis it is apparent that a divine person and a human person are both like and unlike each other. They are like in three ways.

Each possesses a spiritual nature. Each is an individual form of being. Each, too, is incommunicable. Just as Peter cannot share his individuality with John, so the Father cannot share his individuality with the Son or the Spirit. Yet the differences are no less marked. Each human person is a substance in the Aristotelian sense of *prote ousia*. He is one instance of a generic nature who exists in his own right and who is thereby capable of entering into relations with other persons. But each person of the Trinity possesses the whole nature of the Godhead. Each is individuated solely by his relation to the other persons. To this metaphysical difference there corresponds a psychological difference. Each human person is conscious of himself as one who is substantially distinct from other persons. But the members of the divine Triad are conscious of themselves as being indivisibly one.

The question of the self-consciousness possessed by the members of the Triad brings to light the final point of difference between a divine and a human person. In so far as each of the divine persons is distinct from the others he is aware of himself as being thus distinct. Yet he is not aware of being a self in the human sense of the term. Each human person is aware of himself as being one among many instances of humanity. Each too is aware of himself as being a single entity that exists alongside other entities. But each of the divine persons is aware of himself as possessing the whole of the divine nature and as constituting, with the other persons, one, indivisible, God.[11]

If, then, we are to use the terms 'person' and 'self-consciousness' in the senses that are applicable to human beings we must apply them, analogically, to God in his unity, not his triunity. It is the one God who constitutes (to quote from Boethius's well-known definition of a person) an 'individual substance'. Also each of the divine persons is aware of himself as being, though distinct, identical with this one substance. Similarly if we mean by 'personality' one substance (metaphysically) and the awareness of it (psychologically) we must attribute 'personality' to God in his unity.

Because of the difference between a divine person and a human person, and because *hypostasis* in the trinitarian formula does not mean 'person' or 'personality' in our modern sense, it has often been suggested that 'person' be dropped from trinitarian terminology. I do not endorse this suggestion for several reasons. First, 'person' has been used in this context for so long a time that its total abandonment is impossible. Secondly, by retaining it we are reminded of the truth that each member of the Triad wholly expresses in his own way the spiritual nature of the one God. Lastly any other terminology has its own danger. Thus to call the Three modes, or even ways, of being could suggest modalism. I hold, therefore, that we ought to retain 'person' and make the appropriate qualifications.

There are further refinements of trinitarian theology that fall outside the scope of this book. Some of these in any case are very speculative and so cannot be answered with certitude. There is, however, one question that requires consideration on account of its importance in the relation between the Western and the Eastern branches of the Church. This concerns the *filioque* clause. The Niceno-Constantinopolitan creed affirms only that the Spirit proceeds 'from the Father'. In the fifth century the Western Church added 'and from the Son' (*filioque*). This addition has been constantly rejected by the Orthodox Church. Orthodox theologians admit (on scriptural grounds) that within the order of revelation the Spirit is sent by the Son; but they deny that the Spirit proceeds from the Son within the eternal Godhead.

I maintain that the Western view is the correct one. I shall first consider Eastern objections to the *filioque* as these are stated by Timothy Ware in his *The Orthodox Church*.[12] Ware gives three grounds for rejecting the *filioque*. First, by affirming that the Spirit proceeds from the Son as well as the Father Western theologians endanger the 'monarchy' of the Father as the sole source of the Godhead. Secondly, in order to avoid ditheism these theologians affirm that the Spirit proceeds from the Father and the Son 'as from one principle' *tanquam ex uno principio); but this involves a form of Sabellianism whereby the first and second persons of the Trinity 'are merged and confused'. Thirdly, 'as a result of the *filioque* the Holy Spirit in western thought has become subordinated to the Son - if not in theory, then at any rate in practice.'

I do not think that Ware's objections are sound. First, because the Father is the origin of the Son his monarchy cannot be affected by the Spirit's procession from the Son. Secondly, in so far as the Son, though distinct from the Father, fully shares the Father's nature the Spirit can be said to proceed from the Father and the Son 'as from one principle'. Thirdly, although there are grounds for affirming that Western theologians have sometimes neglected belief in the Holy Spirit this neglect is not a logical consequence of *filioque*. The chief reason for assenting to the *filioque* is this. Following Eastern tradition Ware admits that although the Spirit does not proceed from the Son eternally 'so far as the mission of the Spirit to the world is concerned he is sent by the Son and is indeed the "Spirit of the Son".' Ware then quotes John 15. 26 where Christ says that he will send the Paraclete to his disciples. If, then, the Spirit does not proceed eternally from the Son as well as the Father, Christ, in his temporal mission, would not reveal God as he essentially is; and so we should be faced with the objections I have already brought against the severence of the economic from the essential Trinity.

Three other factors can be urged in favour of the *filioque*. First, the only evidence we have for any assertions we make concerning God's essential triunity is the form of his triune revelation. This means that if the Spirit proceeds from the Son economically we have no grounds for affirming that he does not proceed essentially. Secondly, it is inconceivable that the Son could have the capacity to send the Spirit economically unless the Spirit also proceeds from him eternally. Thirdly, Ware admits that Byzantine theologians were willing to speak of 'an eternal manifestation of the Holy Spirit by the Son'. The distinction between 'manifestation' and 'procession' is such a fine one that to me at least it seems to be a distinction without a difference.

Finally, there is the question whether the doctrine of the Trinity is rational. With regard to this doctrine, as with regard to the doctrines of creation and the Incarnation, it is necessary to distinguish between what is supra-rational in the sense of being a mystery beyond our comprehension and what is irrational in the sense that no rational account of it can be given (or, alternatively, in the sense that it fails to satisfy rational criteria). I maintain that the doctrine of the Trinity, like the doctrines of Creation and the Incarnation, while being supra-rational in so far as it signifies an impenetrable mystery, is not irrational. Although we cannot comprehend the Trinity any more than we can comprehend God's creativity and incarnation we can understand it, as we can understand God's creativity and incarnation, sufficiently to perceive that belief in it conforms to rational criteria. The following are my grounds for affirming within these limits the rationality of belief in the Trinity. Since I have already stated the first, second and third grounds I shall now concentrate on the fourth.

1. The belief is firmly based on the New Testament and the creeds. The fact that in the New Testament - and later in the patristic period - belief in the hypostatic character of the Spirit developed more slowly than belief in the hypostatic character of the Son is explicable for the reasons I have given.

2. As I stated in chapter one, the doctrine of the Trinity reconciles the paradoxical affirmations that God is self-sufficient and that he is love. God is self-sufficient love through the inner communion by which he exists as Father, Son and Holy Spirit. His act of creation is a purely altruistic overflowing of this love.

3. The Spirit is required in order to re-present Christ to believers. In himself the human Jesus is, even in his exalted state, incommunicable - the same man as he once was on earth. Yet he is universifiable by virtue of his hypostatic union with the Word. And he is universalized by the Spirit who proceeds eternally from him.

4. The Trinity infinitely expresses an ideal of personal being that we reflect in finite modes. Our existence as persons revolves around two poles: individuality and relationship. Each of us is an individual who as such is distinct from other persons. Yet each of us exists in relation to other persons. Our humanity depends on our success in maintaining a balance between these poles. On the one hand an excessive stress on our individuality impoverishes us by cutting us off from those many forms of spiritual enrichment that communion with other persons

brings. It can also deepen the self-centredness that lies at the root of original sin. On the other hand a fruitful relation with other people depends on the recognition that our individual distinctness makes it impossible for us to become exactly like them or to become identical with them. Hence solitude as well as communion, distance as well as nearness, a sense of otherness as well as a sense of sameness is bound to characterize even the closest friendship.

This polarity is absent from God. Its absence is entailed by the fact of subsistent relations. A divine person is individually distinct solely through his relation to the other persons. This fact is further illuminated by the concept of interpenetration or co-inherence (*perichoresis*). The divine persons, being substantially identical, wholly penetrate and inhere in each other. In these ways the inner life of God differs in kind from the inter-personal lives of his creatures; for each human person can be related to other human persons only because he already exists as a separate entity; and no human person can to any extent inhere in another person, however strongly and closely two persons are united in mutual love.

In differing thus from his creatures God expresses personality in an uncreated mode that shows its infinite perfection by the manner in which it transcends the polarity that characterizes human modes. This perfection was stated thus by Paul Henry (who has in mind especially Augustine's presentation of trinitarianism). 'God is the perfect, in fact the only perfect, prototype of that which all love between persons tends to achieve - absolute unity and yet distinction - to be one with the other, not by losing one's identity but by perfecting it, even at the very source of one's being. That is why divine existence is the ideal of all personal existence - to be fully oneself, but only in dependence upon, and in adherence to, another in the communion of unity.'[13]

The Trinity, then, is (to use Platonic terms) the archetype of personality that human persons 'copy' or 'imitate'. This is an inevitable consequence of the fact that man is made in God's image. I offer two concluding comments.

First, although both the psychological and the social analogies of the Trinity exhibit finite forms of a unity-in-diversity that exists infinitely in God the social analogy is necessary in order to complete the psychological one because it shows that we reflect the Trinity not merely as individuals but also in our relation to each other. We are by nature social beings because we are created reflections of the divine society that is constituted by the Father, the Son and the Holy Spirit.

Secondly, a further Platonic concept is that of 'participation'. The Christian significance of the concept within this context is as follows. We reflect God's triunity by nature; we participate in it only by grace - through the action of the Holy Spirit in uniting us with the incarnate and exalted Son in his self-offering to the Father. I shall discuss this participation in chapter six.

22-3). Kelly comments that 'the trinitarian ground-plan obtrudes itself obstinately throughout, and its presence is all the more striking because more often than not there is nothing in the context to necessitate it' (p 23).

[3] The article on 'Spirit' in Kittel's *Worterbuch* (English trans., London 1960, p. 1).

[4] J. Lebreton, *History of the Dogmas of the Trinity* (English trans., London 1939, p 82).

[5] In the volume he edited, *Essays on the Trinity and the Incarnation* (London 1928).

[6] p 168.

[7] pp 171-2.

[8] Some theologians have affirmed that Christ was not (or not merely) an individual man but that he was, generically, Man. Certainly it is valid to call Christ 'Man' in so far as he was the ideal man (man as he ought to be), the representative man (who, through his perfect sacrifice, presents us to the Father) and the head of a new creation. Yet he himself is individual; for universals do not exist outside their instances unless they exist (as Plato held) *per se* in an eternal realm or (as some Christian theologians have held) as ideas in the mind of God. In any case if Christ's humanity was not concrete he would not have been consubstantial with us; but to affirm that his humanity was both concrete and universal is (so it seems to me) self-contradictory. Furthermore, God could not impart his ubiquity to the individual humanity of the exalted Christ (according to the Lutheran understanding of *communicatio idiomatum);* for such an impartation would destory the finiteness that is an essential characteristic of humanity. Yet because Christ's humanity exists solely in union with the Word, and because within this union God activates it supernaturally, it possesses a capacity for universal communication. The view that the Spirit is the one who conveys the life-giving power of Christ's risen life to believers conforms wholly to the teaching of the N.T. Thus Moule affirms, with reference to Acts and the fourth gospel, that 'the Spirit communicates and extends the presence of Christ' (op. cit. p 104). Among those theologians who have stressed this function of the Spirit Calvin deserves special note. He insists that although Christ 'can always be present with his people breathing into them his own life' he is thus present through the Spirit who proceeds from him. (Inst. 4. 17). Calvin earlier summed it up thus in speaking of divine grace and its benefits: 'The whole comes to this, that the Holy Spirit is the bond by which Christ effectually binds us to himself' (3. 1).

[9] *Church Dogmatics* (English trans., *The Doctrine of the Word of God,* Edinburgh 1936, p 420).

[10] *In the Image and Likeness of God* (St. Vladimir's Seminary Press, 1974, p 79).

[11] There are two reasons for affirming that each of the divine persons is self-conscious. First, all orthodox exponents of trinitarianism must admit that the persons are united by mutual knowledge and love; but such a union would be impossible without self-consciousness. Secondly, it is also an axiom or trinitarianism that the Father, the Son and the Spirit are all, equally, God. And so each must possess the whole nature of the Godhead in respect of every personal property (including self-consciousness). However, these three forms of consciousness are not separate, as they would be for three men. Because each member of the Triad is aware of himself only in relation to the others and is also aware of himself as possessing wholly the nature possessed by the others we must affirm ultimately with Karl Rahner that 'there is only one real consciousness in God, which is shared by Father, Son and Spirit, by each in his own proper way' (*The Trinity,* London 1970, p 107). In a footnote on the same page Rahner quotes Lonergan with approval for the view that 'the three subjects are aware of each other through one consciousness which is possessed in a different way by the three of them'.

[12] London 1963, pp 218-23.

[13] *St. Augustine on Personality* (New York 1960, p 10).

CHAPTER 4
PROVIDENCE AND PRAYER

The idea of providence has three main elements: omniscience, control and care. To believe in divine providence is to affirm or at least to imply that God knows all events, that he has complete control of them, and that he cares for the world he has created.

1. God knows all events. What, then, is the mode of his knowledge? Here there are two main views. According to classical theism (as expressed in the writings of Aquinas) God knows all events as occurring timelessly in a mode that corresponds to his own timeless mode of being. Other theologians and philosophers assert that even if God himself exists timelessly he knows the world in its objectively real successiveness. He knows events, not only as present, but also as past and future. If we hold the first view we cannot speak, except as a deliberate concession to our finite perspective, of divine foreknowledge; but if we hold the second view we can so speak, although of course only within the limits of analogical predication.

I shall leave the choice between these views open. The only question with which I am now concerned is whether God's knowledge of his creatures is complete and so whether he is omniscient. Obviously according to the first view God is omniscient. As the Creator he knows completely every creature if it is presented immediately to his vision. The problem that arises from the second view concerns the extent of God's foreknowledge. There is no difficulty in supposing that he could foreknow completely all purely physical events that are predictable. Yet could he foreknow freely chosen human acts? I do not see how he could do so because such acts are inherently unpredictable. However, the absence of foreknowledge on God's part here would not endanger belief in either his omniscience or his omnipotence. The first belief is not endangered; for even God can know only what is knowable. The second belief is not endangered; for God would foreknow every possible choice, and he could assimilate all choices to his sovereign will.[1]

2. God controls all events. His control is twofold. He normally controls the world of physical nature by the properties and laws with which he originally endowed it. I say 'normally' because I wish to leave room for the possibility that he sometimes intervenes miraculously in nature. He controls human beings by eliciting from them a free choice between obeying and disobeying his will. It has been objected that if men can disobey God they are to that extent independent of him, and that he to that extent lacks control over them. The answer to this objection is that man's free will is itself a gift from God. It is among the highest gifts he confers on his spiritual creatures. Also it lies wholly

within his right and power to judge men in another world according to the choices they have made one earth.

Because God deals with men by persuasion, not compulsion - by cooperating with their free decisions, not by imposing his own will on them - the whole concept of predestination is unacceptable. By this concept I mean the belief that God predestines some men to salvation and others to damnation by a hidden decree that no human mind can comprehend. Augustine's attempts to reconcile predestination with, on the one hand, God's goodness and, on the other hand, man's free will are wholly unconvincing. It is, however, important to distinguish between the concept of predestination and the concept of election. The second concept can be interpreted in ways that are compatible with the concept of free will. To say that God elects a person for salvation or for some special task is consonant with saying that the person is free to accept or to reject God's choice. The outstanding example is Israel. Although God chose Israel as the instrument of his saving purpose many Jews rejected his choice. Only a remnant remained faithful. Whether it is theologically fruitful to extend the concept of election beyond Israel and Christ (considered as the 'elect one' in whom God's purpose for Israel was fulfilled) is a further question. My only point now is that the concept can be extended without infringing belief in human freedom.

This belief also compels us to be wary of interpreting the idea of providence through the idea of a divine plan. As soon as we start to speak of such a 'plan' we are apt to understand it in terms of a detailed history that God envisages for the future of either an individual or a social group. We are then compelled to affirm either that God will impose his plan on men whatever happens or that he will adapt his plan to their free choices. I have already rejected the first affirmation which is a concealed form of predestinarianism. The difficulty in the second is that because there are so many human choices entailing so many consequences we must attribute so many modifications to God's plan that the idea of a single plan disintegrates. I therefore suggest that we either abandon the concept of a divine plan or restrict its reference to God's general, eschatological, plan of salvation which is to unite all mankind in Christ.

3. This element in the idea of providence needs no comment. God cares for the world that he created out of selfless, purely altruistic, love. In particular he cares for each human person whom he has created in his image and thereby fashioned for eternal life with him. Yet here we encounter the whole, vast, problem of evil that I shall discuss in the next chapter.

This, then, is the essence of Christian belief in providence. I shall now examine three questions that it raises. I shall deal briefly with the first and second because the answers to them, while being capable of indefinite expansion are, I believe, in outline clear. Also the third question is most apt to cause difficulty and misunderstanding.

Furthermore, it is closely related to problems inherent in petitionary and intercessory prayer.

1. Is it possible to discern God's providence in nature? An affirmative answer can be given by pointing to the data assembled in the factual premiss of the telelogical argument for theism. Whether these data compel an inference to God on the part of those who do not antecedently believe in him is a question of natural theology with which I am not here concerned. But they undoubtedly confirm a faith that is already present. Nature's order and stability, the emergence of the higher from the lower in the course of evolution, the correspondence between mind and its physical environment, the existence of beauty in modes far exceeding biological needs all indicate God's wisdom and power. More particularly, our knowledge of the evolutionary process permits us to affirm that God's final purpose in creating our world was to produce man in whom all the preceding stages of both mind and matter are simultaneously transcended and summed up. Yet however far we continue these reflections we are sooner or later brought up against two facts that seem to militate against the belief that the Designer of the universe is infinite both in power and in love. First, there are the manifold forms of suffering that the world of nature inflicts. Secondly, man, when physically considered, is only an evanescent speck in a desert of lifeless stars. And so the consideration of God's providence in nature needs to be supported by belief in immortality and in the revelation of his love in Christ.

2. Can we discern God's providence in history? This question can be reformulated more precisely thus. Does history bear marks of a divine purpose? The answer we give to this question depends on the meaning we attach to 'purpose'. If we take it to mean that God's purpose for men is that they should obey his will and imitate his character the answer must be that history provides *some* evidence that his purpose is being fulfilled. The chief evidence for Christians is constituted by the lives of the saints (among whom I include all whose sanctity, especially when proved through suffering, is conspicuous). Yet the contrary evidence provided by evil persons and the harm they do is often apt to strike us as being greater.

However, the concept of a divine purpose in this context is usually taken to mean that the course of history itself shows signs of being directed by God towards the goal that he intends for it. All Christians are obliged to hold that they can discern a special, redemptive, purpose of God in the so-called 'sacred history' of Israel when this is viewed in the light of Christ whom it prefigures and in whom it is fulfilled. Many Christians would wish to add that there is a special preparation for the Gospel (*praeparatio evangelii*) in the civilizations of Greece and Rome. Yet the farther we move from Christian origins the less able we become to see a divine purpose in history. In particular we are unable to perceive any universal progress towards the establishment of the ideal society that God intends for mankind. This failure of perception is objectively caused by three facts: the fact of human sinfulness (that can reach demonic proportions in the political sphere), the fact that God continues to respect human freedom however much it may be abused, and the fact that God's Kingdom or Reign is eschatological in character. The first and second of these facts need no amplification; but the third needs stressing. According to the New Testament the divine Reign that Christ inaugurated will be fulfilled only at his last 'coming' (*parousia*) 'in a new heaven and a new earth'.

The enigmatic nature of historical events in relation to God's will affects even the history of the Church. In its essence the Church is a supernatural community that is commissioned to proclaim and embody the redemptive ministry of its Lord. As such its unique and transcendent place among earthly institutions is assured. Yet it is composed of sinners who by their spiritual blindness, arrogance and self-seeking fail to execute fully God's purpose for it. Also almost from the beginning it has been inextricably involved in secular structures that impede as much as help the discharge of its function. Hence even it does not exhibit an unfolding copy of divine perfection. It awaits a final transformation in the Kingdom of God that is yet to come.

The difficulty involved in detecting a divine purpose in the history of both secular and ecclesiastical institutions can be illustrated by many examples of which I choose the following. On the secular side it seemed to many Christians at the begining of this century that the growth of Western civilization and in particular of liberal democracy was a divinely guided process that approximated to, even if it was not identical with, the advent of God's Kingdom on earth. This view was shattered by the horrors of World War 1. It may be said that at any rate the Western democracies' victory over Nazism in World War 2 showed divine providence operating negatively in the form of judgment on evil. Yet counter-evidence can be produced. Someone could say that the suffering inflicted by the Nazis was beyond remedy or compensation; that the communist form of totalitarianism which was strengthened by World War 2 is as evil as the Nazi form; and that since 1945 Western democracies have shown increasing signs of disintegration. On the ecclesiastical side I choose the Reformation as my example. Protestants are naturally tempted to say that it was providential that Luther arose to oppose the errors of the late medieval church and to recall Christians to the purity of the Gospel. Yet a host of questions remains.

I mention only two. Would it not have been better if the Pope had been more conciliatory and Luther less vehement so that the schism between Catholics and Protestants could have been avoided? Again, was Luther's interpretation of the Gospel wholly pure? It is arguable that the Tridentine decrees are in some respects closer to the teaching of the New Testament.

In raising these queries concerning our attempts to perceive divine providence in history I do not of course wish to deny (what every Christian must regard as a matter of faith) that God is purposively active in secular as well as ecclesiastical institutions. I mean only to affirm that we cannot decode his purpose. We cannot do so for the reasons I have given. First, his purpose does not take the form of a plan that he imposes on events, and that can be inferred from them. Secondly, he permits evil acts and their consequences in order to co-operate with our free decisions. Thirdly, his only final purpose and fixed 'plan' is to fulfil all things in an end and goal that transcend the confines of this present world.

In any case God's purpose in history ultimately concerns persons, not institutions. His purpose is to prepare human souls for heavenly communion with him and so, derivatively, with each other. Institutions change and will ultimately disappear; but God's purpose for persons is unchanging, and they are, at least potentially, eternal. And so I pass to the third question that the concept of providence raises.

3. Is God's providence discernible in individual lives? Here we must distinguish between a general and a particular sense that 'providence' can bear. In general we can sometimes be confident in detecting the operations of providence in the direction that people's lives have taken. Certainly we cannot detect it in material benefits that God confers as a reward for virtue or in material penalties that he attaches to vice. Yet we can sometimes detect it on the spiritual plane. An outstanding example is the conversion of Augustine as he records it in his Confessions. Many of us have witnessed other, lesser, examples of God's redeeming grace. A person can also speak, at least in retrospect, of God's providence operating in his own life. Thus he can claim to have received a progressively sharpened sense of his dependence on God, of being constantly sustained in hope and of being somehow guided along the way of salvation in spite of his sins and folly.

However, when people speak of divine providence in a personal context they often mean something more specific. They mean that some events are in a special and particular sense providential. Thus we say 'it was providential' that X occurred or that it did not occur. Sometimes such statements are made loosely by unbelievers. But when they are made genuinely by believers they signify the conviction that these events are in some special way signs of God's universal providence. Are there such events? Before this question can be answered two distinctions must be drawn.

First, we must distinguish between objective and subjective interpretations of events. According to the objective interpretation God actually determines events in specially providential ways that are in themselves different from the says in which he normally governs the world. Each specially providential act is thus distinct from his general providence in its *modus operandi*. According to the subjective interpretation when we call an act specially providential we mean merely that *for us* it is a special sign of God's general providence. The second distinction is between physical events and events that, though having physical conditions and effects, are mentally caused and so can be called 'personal' events.

I shall begin with the objective interpretation of physical events in terms of a special providence. Here it is necessary to refer to the idea of the miraculous. In chapter one I defined a miracle as 'an unusual event of a physical or material kind that supersedes the laws of nature and is due to a supernatural act of God'. The question I now wish to ask is this. Are some acts of God specially providential without being miraculous? I do not think so. I find it impossible to envisage an intermediate class of events between those that are instances of uniform laws and those that are miraculously caused by a supernatural act of God.

It has been suggested that we can posit such a class of events on the ground of quantum physics according to which the ultimate particles of matter operate in a random fashion that can be predicted in terms of statistical probability but not of rigid laws. Hence (so the suggestion goes) God could intervene in the movement of basic particles in such a way as to produce one result rather than another. This result could therefore be called specially providential. I maintain that this suggestion is vulnerable to the following criticisms. First, if the behaviour of nature's basic elements were one day to be explained by causal laws there would be no scope for God to act in this way. Secondly, even if there is an irremovable element of indeterminacy at the microcosmic level, casual laws still operate at the macrocosmic level accessible to normal observation. At the latter level any exception to established laws would be regarded either as an anomaly requiring a re-examination of the law or as a miracle.

Let us next consider the possibility of God acting in a specially providential way in personal events. In so far as these are physically conditioned they are covered by what I have just said. The question now is whether God thus acts in their mental aspects. It may be held that he specially inspires persons to speak or act in ways that are specially providential. Here, I maintain, the distinction between the general and the particular, rules and exceptions to them, is inapplicable. All God's acts in and towards the soul are special, and so all the physical events they indirectly cause are also special. God never treats human beings (as he treats entities in nature) merely as instances of a universal law. He always adapts himself to them out of his unfailing wisdom and love. When they are open to his presence he influences them in modes suited to their good. When they are not thus open he awaits their response according to his infinite patience. Here we can easily apply the principle of analogy and the *via eminentiae*. If even we are capable of adapting ourselves to the individual needs of those whom we encounter how much more must this be true of God.

I therefore conclude that whenever we describe a non-miraculous event as specially providential (by contrast with other events that we do not thus describe) we can validly do so only in a subjective sense. The most we are entitled to claim is that from our point of view this or that is a special sign of God's providence. Moreover, we can say this much only in a provisional way because of the following facts. First, the final meaning of every event lies in two unspecifiable consequences. These are our future free responses to the event and the fulfilment of the event, together with our lives as a whole, in the Kingdom of God. Secondly, any attempt to interpret events in terms of God's providential care for us leads, unless we are careful, to self-centredness. Others, even with the best religious intentions and motives, may not see signs of providence in the same events in relation to their own lives. What seems a blessing to one may seem a curse to another. Lastly we must always remember that God's illumination and inspiration are always hidden; they are never immediately perceptible even to the eye of faith.

I shall illustrate these principles by three examples. Let us consider first a person who is the sole survivor in an air crash. If he is religious it is natural for him to regard his survival as providential. Yet he cannot validly use the adjective in an objective sense. Unless his survival was a miracle it, like the deaths of the other passengers, was inexorably caused by material factors. In the context of the aircraft's mechanical failure he survived because he was sitting in a safe place whereas the others died because they were sitting in vulnerable places. Even if he uses the word 'providential' subjectively he must remember that an opposite judgment will be made by the relatives of those who were killed; that he is entitled to regard his own survival as a special sign of God's providence only if he is truly grateful for it and so makes it an occasion for re-dedicating his life to God; and that God is no less actively concerned for those who died.

My second example is taken from the sphere of human agency. Let us imagine a person A who suddenly feels impelled to speak to a stranger B. Let us also imagine that B was on the verge of committing suicide but was prevented by A's words. Obviously both A and B will regard the encounter as providential. Yet even here we must bear in mind factors I have mentioned. We cannot perceive God's inspiration or, therefore, describe its mode in this or any other case. Chiefly we must not regard either A's words or B's response as objectively, in an exclusive sense, providential. Every word of comfort or encouragement is, for believers, a particular and unrepeated sign of God's activity in the lives of men. Also God is equally present in his saving power with both those who do and those who do not find a friend in time of need.

My last example is a claim to see God's providence in a coincidence of mental and physical factors producing an especially favourable result (such as a happy marriage or a merited promotion in one's career). We must interpret these coincidences also subjectively and with the qualifications I mentioned. An objective interpretation is absurd. Quite apart from the criticisms I have already made it would imply that God manipulates physical laws and even human persons in order to secure what at any moment we consider to be to our advantage. Surely the truth is that God permits coincidences as part of his universal providence. His particular providence consists, first in his invitation to each one of us to seek his will in all circumstances, and secondly in his forgiveness of us when through our own fault we have failed to discern or obey his will.

It has been said that all events are equally providential. There are two senses in which this is true. Both put what I have said in perspective. First in all events God's knowledge, control and care are absolute and unvarying. Secondly, therefore, nothing falls outside his sovereignty. There is no evil from which he cannot bring good, and there is no good from which he cannot bring a greater good. The second of these truths was incomparably expressed by Paul in the eighth chapter of his epistle to the Romans. 'We know', he says in verse 28, 'that in everything God works for good with those who love him, who are called according to his purpose.'

In order to understand Paul rightly we must note the following points.

(i) Paul did not base his claim on an inference from nature or history. He did not base it even on God's revelation to Israel. He based it solely on the love of God revealed in Christ. And so he concludes this magnificent chapter thus. 'For I am sure that neither death, nor life, nor angels, nor principalities, nor things to come, nor powers, nor height, nor depth, nor anything else in all creation, will be able to separate us from the love of God in Christ Jesus our Lord.'

(ii) Paul asserts that God works for good 'with those who love him, who are called according to his purpose'. He thus excludes the view that God's providence operates for believers and for unbelievers in the same way. Only those who love God have a right to claim that he is working *with* them, as one friend with another. Moreover although God overrules evil and produces good within the lives of those who love him he does not overrule their freedom. He cooperates with them for their good.

(iii) Although Paul does not define the 'good' of which he speaks we can infer from his teaching as a whole that he meant two things by it. First, it does not consist in temporal benefits; it is of a spiritual and supernatural kind. It consists in the total transformation of the believer by the Spirit of Christ. Secondly, although the transformation begins in this life it will not be complete until the life to come.

(iv) We cannot unravel God's transforming activity or, therefore, perceive the relation between it and either, on the one hand, the circumstances of our present life or, on the other hand, our final state in the life to come. Here two further affirmations made by Paul in two other epistles are relevant. The first is 'for we walk by faith not by sight'.[2] The second comes from the famous hymn to charity. 'For now we see in a mirror dimly, but then face to face. Now I know in part; then I shall understand fully, even as I have been fully understood.'[3]

Two general conclusions emerge from this brief survey of Paul's teaching on providence.

First, Christians must interpret the concept of providence christologically. The idea of providence is normally related to the idea of creation. This relation obviously exists and it must constantly be borne in mind. God's knowledge of, control of and care for the world are all grounded in the fact that he created it *ex nihilo* in order that it might be a finite reflection of his glory. Yet Christ completes our understanding of providence in the following ways.

(a) As the incarnation of the eternal Word Christ is the supreme expression of God's glory and the ideal of perfect humanity that we are called to imitate and in which, through the Holy Spirit, we are also called to participate. Moreover union with Christ is not a spiritual option reserved for a few while the majority exist outside it. It is the destiny that God intends for all men and so is the goal of his providential activity among them.

(b) Christ is the supreme instance of God bringing good out of evil and bringing out of good an even greater good. The evil of the Crucifixion needs no retelling. Yet out of it and because of it Christ rose from the dead and so proved himself to be victorious over sin and death. Perhaps it is not so obvious that through the Cross God brought out of good a yet greater good. Yet he did so. There could not be any greater spiritual and moral good in terms of human volition than Christ's obedience that led him to accept death on a cross. Yet in terms of divine providence there was a still greater good - namely, a reward for the obedience. Christ recieved this reward when he obtained the glory of his exalted state.

(c) Christ is the final proof of God's love for us. Every attempt to prove God's love from nature and history founders on the fact of evil. Christ, however, proves it in two ways. First, the incarnation is itself an unsurpassable expression of God's love; for God could not show his love more clearly than by living and dying as man for man's sake. Secondly by raising and exalting Christ God revealed conclusively that eternal life is the reward for all who put their trust in him.

(d) Christ both taught his disciples to trust in God's providence and exemplified such trust in his own life. I am especially concerned to stress his exemplification of it. The human Jesus, like every other man, walked by faith and not by sight. Even he did not perceive in unclouded vision his Father's will and action. Even he could not know the outcome of his ministry. Even he, in his final rejection and agony, felt that God's presence was withdrawn. Yet he trusted in God to the end and sealed his life with the words: 'Father into thy hands I commend my spirit'.[4]

Secondly, Christians must interpret God's providence eschatologically. The meaning of our lives will not be finally disclosed until the end when God will fulfil all things in Christ. We cannot have a preliminary glimpse of this future consummation. Our task is to do our duty in accordance with our best understanding (which will never amount to a complete understanding) of God's will in the sure hope that he will produce from our imperfect obedience a supernatural good that we cannot imagine or conceive. This truth was stated thus by *De Caussade* in the following passage in his *Self-Abandonment to Divine Providence*.[5]

When the soul is in health, all goes well, for what comes from God, i.e. the share his action takes in the work, corresponds to the precise degree of the soul's fidelity. God's share is the right side of the work which proceeds in its achievement like those magnificent pieces of tapestry which are composed point by point on the reverse side. The workman employed on them sees nothing but the point on which he is working and his needle, and these points successively filled make up those magnificent figures which only appear when, at the completion of all the parts, the right side is displayed, although during the time of the work all this marvellous beauty is in obscurity.

So is it with the self-abandoned soul; she sees nothing but God and her duty. The accomplishment of this duty is at each moment but an imperceptible point added to the work, and yet it is with these points that God works his wonders of which we have now and then a presentiment in the time of our pilgrimage, but which will only be known in the great day of eternity.

I shall now examine the relevance of these remarks on providence to prayer in its petitionary and intercessory forms. But first I shall state two principles that ought to govern our understanding of prayer as a whole.

First, we must not think that we can inform God of facts of which he would otherwise be ignorant or that through our prayers he is enabled to obtain a clearer vision of our well-being. The ignorance is all on our side and not at all on his. Secondly, we must not think in terms of asking God to change his mind or to adopt a more favourable attitutde towards us. God's will is always set on our good. The aim of prayer is not to conform God's will to our wills but to confirm our wills to his will. Hence whenever we ask him for something to happen we must always qualify our request with the words: 'if it is in accordance with thy will'. This qualification was added by Jesus himself in the prayer that he offered on the eve of his passion: 'Abba, Father, all things are possible to thee; remove this cup from me; yet not what I will but what thou wilt'.[6]

In the light of these two principles there is no problem in asking God to grant us virtues that are necessary for the Christian life and to illumine us in our attempts to discern the good. We know that the granting of these gifts is always in accordance with his will. Hence in asking him for them we are merely expressing our desire to obey his will and opening our souls to the influence of his Spirit. Difficulty arises over (a) intercessions (that is, prayers for the welfare of other people), (b) prayers for physical events within the natural order, and (c) prayers for events depending on the volition of other people. In all these cases the difficulty is to see what difference prayer can make.

(a) In so far as intercessions involve prayers for the *material* welfare of other people I shall cover them under (b). I am now concerned with prayers for the *spiritual* welfare of others. What effect can such prayer have, and so what difference can it make? God is always seeking the spiritual good of other people, just as he is always seeking our own spiritual good. We cannot persuade him to seek their good more efficaciously. I therefore suggest that we interpret such intercessions as ways in which we identify ourselves with God's will for other people and offer ourselves, where this is possible, as means through which his will can operate.

(b) The difficulty here concerns prayers for physical events of a non-miraculous kind. Can we meaningfully ask God to cause an event that occurs according to the normal laws of nature? I shall begin by considering the solution of the problem proposed by C. S. Lewis in his book entitled *Miracles*.[7] Lewis begins by denying (as I have denied) the existence of specially providential, but non-miraculous, events in nature. At the same time he holds that our prayers can be part causes even of non-miraculous events that are physically necessitated. God, in his view, knows all events in a timeless present, a *Totum Simul*. From within this present he adapts necessary sequences so that they coincide with those of our petitions that he chooses to grant. He thus determines a whole sequence from t1 to t9 so that it coincides with petitions offered at t10. Hence Lewis writes thus concerning the result of a battle or a medical consultation. 'The event certainly has been decided - in a sense it was decided "before all worlds". But one of the things taken into account in deciding it, and therefore one of the things that really cause it to happen, may be this very prayer that we are now offering. Thus, shocking as it may sound, I conclude that we can at noon become part causes of an event occurring at ten a.m.'[8]

I find Lewis's view unacceptable on two grounds. First, it is far from certain that even if God is timeless in his own being he knows events timelessly. One can, I believe, consistently hold that even if he is timeless *per se* he knows events in their temporal successiveness, and that he is ignorant of free human choices (including, therefore, prayers) that are yet to be made. Secondly, I cannot see how even an omniscient mind could adjust uniform and necessitated sequences in any significant way to the vast multiplicity of persons and the even vaster multiplicity of their requests. A further observation is relevant. Even when full account has been taken of the fact that all God's answers to prayers are unverifiable, the further fact that natural calamities often envelop men indiscriminately tends to falsify, or at least to make intolerably enigmatic, a divine adjustment of necessitated sequences to human prayers.

However, we cannot simply jettison petitions for material gifts. To do so would run counter to the continuous practice of Christians and to the explicit teaching of Jesus who included a petition for daily bread in the prayer he gave to his disciples. Let us note too that Jesus regarded this petition as being fully in accordance with belief in God's universal providence. Thus soon after the Lord's Prayer in Matthew's gospel he commands his listeners not to be anxious about what they shall eat and drink; for 'your heavenly Father knows that you need them all'.[9] Similarly earlier in the sermon he refers to God as one who 'makes his sun rise on the evil and on the good, and sends rain on the just and the unjust'.[10]

I suggest that we can validly pray for material benefits that fall within the normal order of nature if we interpret our prayers as requests that God should continue to show his goodness towards us. Certainly we must avoid any suggestion that by our petitions we can persuade him to display a generosity that would otherwise not be forthcoming. Also we must not think that by a concealed qualification he has decided to make the continuance of nature's order dependent on our prayers. He is always infinitely generous, and his will in relation to the future of the universe is necessarily inscrutable. In asking him for material gifts we are expressing our total dependence on him in the future as well as the present and the past. It is the future reference that justifies the petitionary form and distinguishes the prayer from an act of thanksgiving for a gift that has already been bestowed. To put the same point negatively and with reference to the Lord's Prayer, the petition for our daily bread is a wholly appropriate way of excluding any tendency to think that we can take God's gifts for granted or claim them as our right. Hence Christians find it wholly natural to offer the petition even when they believe fully in God's antecedent providence and even when they have assented fully to the scientific understanding of nature in terms of regular sequences and causal laws.

Yet it seems to me that we cannot validly ask God for variations within natural sequences without at the same time asking him for a miracle. Thus although everyone can validly pray for daily bread in the general sense of asking God to continue those natural sequences by which bread is produced no one can thus validly ask him to interrupt those sequences non-miraculously (for example, by non-miraculously sending rain that would not otherwise come in a famine-struck area). Similarly, although we can validly pray for the recovery of sick persons in the general sense of asking God to continue the curative processes of nature we cannot validly ask him to interrupt those processes non-miraculously (for example, by non-miraculously healing a person who has reached the terminal stage of cancer).

(c) A further difficulty arises over praying for events that would be due to the volitions of other people. What can such prayers effect? We cannot expect God to violate another person's freedom or suddenly change that person's disposition in order that the person should act according to our requests. Also we cannot ask God to be more closely present to a person or to act more effectively in him; for God's moral presence is infinite and unvarying.

I conclude that we ought to be very reluctant to pray for the occurrence or non-occurrence of particular events. I doubt whether we should ever offer such a prayer unless it is wrenched from us in agony (as Christ's prayer to be spared the Cross was wrenched from him). Then, provided we qualify the prayer (as Christ qualified it) with the words 'if it is in accordance with thy will', God will accept the prayer and answer it as he sees fit. Directly, in terms of the petition itself, the answer may well be the negative one that Christ himself received. Yet indirectly it will consist in the experience of God's power in enabling us (as it enabled Christ) to endure a trial that is inevitable.

Two comments will, I hope, put what I have just said in a final perspective.

First, if we are in doubt concerning the propriety of a particular request we need not use a petitionary form of words. It is enough to 'commit' ourselves or others to God or to 'remember' others before him. Such a 'committing' and 'remembering' in any case belong to the essence of petitionary and intercessory prayer. If we want to use a petitionary form of words it is enough simply to ask God to help us or others in this or that situation according to his will.

Secondly, all prayer must pass beyond petition and intercession to thanksgiving and submission. We must always thank God for all his gifts, and above all for the gift of his unbroken presence. Also we must always submit ourselves wholly to him in the knowledge that he cooperates with those who love him for their good according to the pattern of his self-revelation in Christ.

[1] I have argued elsewhere, on the one hand that God himself is timeless, but on the other hand that he knows the world in its temporal sequence; so that he is ignorant of future free choices (*Concepts of Deity*, pp 19-22, 30-33). However, I must add two qualifications. First, although I still adhere to the view that God is eternal in the sense of being timeless, it is religiously sufficient to affirm (according to the definition of God's eternity I gave in chapter one) that he is eternal simply in the sense that he is without beginning and without end; for this affirmation differentiates him from all creatures and, when taken together with the affirmation of his other attributes, justifies worship of him. The believer can be contentedly agnostic concerning further interpretations of God's eternity in terms of either endless time or timelessness. Secondly - and this is the point that is immediately relevant here - it is religiously sufficient to affirm that God knows allthings; for this affirmation, again when taken together with the affirmation of his other attributes, is enough tojustify trust in him. The believer can be contentedly agnostic concerning any statements that are made concerning the mode of God's knowledge. And one can affirm the fact of God's omniscience on the basis of belief in him as the Creator. If he created the world *ex nihilo* he must know it to the full extent that it is, by his own will, knowable.

[2] 2 Cor. 5. 7.
[3] 1 Cor. 13. 12.
[4] Lk. 23. 46.
[5] English trans., London 1955, pp 125-6.
[6] Mk. 14. 36.
[7] London 1960.
[8] p 183.
[9] Mt. 6. 32.
[10] Mt. 5. 45.

CHAPTER 5
EVIL

In discussing the problem constituted by the presence of evil in a world created by an almighty God of love the theist must be guided by the following complementary facts. On the one hand so long as he has faith he will believe that the problem is soluble. On the other hand he is obliged for three reasons to work out the solution as fully and as rationally as possible. First, faith is by nature 'faith seeking understanding' (*fides quaerens intellectum*). Secondly, to an agnostic evil is bound to constitute the chief evidence against belief in God. Thirdly, even a person who has faith can lose it if he is unable to reconcile it with the fact of evil or to cope with evil when he encounters it in his own life.

Writers on the problem are accustomed to distinguish between 'moral' and 'physical' (or 'natural') forms of evil. This distinction is valid. A 'moral' evil is an evil disposition shown by or an evil act performed by a human person. A 'physical' evil belongs to the order of nature and is one for which no human person is responsible. Examples of the first form are greed, sensuality and murder. Examples of the second are disease, earthquakes and floods. Of course these forms can overlap. Thus disease can be caused by man's negligence or folly. Yet the forms are often independent of each other, and so they must be considered separately.

In tackling the problem I shall distinguish between four further aspects of it: (a) the origin of evil, (b) the justification of evil solely in terms of this world and without an appeal to Christian revelation, (c) evil's cure considered in terms of both the life to come and Christian revelation, and (d) the final justification of evil in terms of this cure. I shall begin by considering (a) and (b) in relation to, first, moral evil and, secondly, physical evil.

Two explanations of sin's origin seem to me to be untenable. First, its origin has been identified with Adam's 'fall'. Adam 'fell' by a deliberate transgression of God's command; and his sinfulness was communicated to all his descendants. Although this view has deeply influenced Christian thought it is exposed to two objections. First, the biological theory of evolution makes it very difficult to envisage a 'first man' who possessed the intellectual and moral maturity that the view presupposes. Secondly, even if such a person did exist it is impossible to understand how, if he was perfect, he could sin; for the ability to sin implies the existence of evil inclinations. John Hick states the objection thus. 'The notion that man was at first spiritually and morally good, orientated in love towards his Maker, and free to express his flawless nature without even the hindrance of contrary temptations, and yet that he preferred to be evil and miserable, cannot be saved from the charge of self-contradiction and absurdity.'[1]

The second explanation, if true, would provide an answer to the second objection. It has been maintained that because man is a mutable and contingent being he is bound to sin. Thus Hick quotes a Thomist theologian, P. M. Farrell, as saying that 'evil is involved in the very concept and definition of contingent being.' Hick then offers the following comments that I endorse. 'There are, however, two reasons for being dissatisfied with this argument. First (as Marvin Zimmermann has pointed out in a note on Farrell's article), Farrell slides from contingency as entailing the possibility of ceasing to exist, to contingency as entailing the possibility of (existing but) ceasing to be good. He establishes a point concerning contingency in the first sense, and then assumes, illegitimately, that he has established it concerning contingency in the second sense. And, secondly, Farrell slides from the necessary *possibility* of defection from good to the necessary *fact* of defection from good, and concludes that evil (and not only the possibility of evil) is a necessary consequence of contingency.'[2]

A more plausible view was held by William Temple. He traced the origin of sin to the fact that man is a finite and self-conscious being endowed with imagination. Because man is finite it was likely that he would see things primarily from his own standpoint and so seek his own good in preference to the good of others. 'As soon as consciousness advances to full self-consciousness, so that the self, distinguishing itself from its environment, not only chooses what appetites it shall satisfy but even what ends it shall pursue, self-centredness becomes self-assertion. The good-for-self is alone effectively apparent good, and good in a fuller sense, though recognized to be real, is relatively powerless as a motive. It is not utterly necessary that this should be so; and therefore it is not true to say that God made man selfish, or predestined him to sin. But that it should be so was "too probable not to happen"; and it is true to say that God so made the world that man was likely to sin, and the dawn of moral consciousness was likely to be more of a "fall" than an ascent.'[3] This process was aided by the imagination 'which not only stimulates desire beyond its proper province, so that it becomes lust, but also, being specially responsive to fear, exaggerates the peril proceeding from the rivalries and antagonisms of the competing individuals and groups, poisoning all thought and feeling with rancour and bitterness'.[4] And once aggressiveness arose in even one man it would propagate itself in others through imitation and self-defence.

Temple's account of sin's origin seems to me to be convincing when it is related to three further facts. First, man's original struggle with physical nature inevitably sharpened his sense of self-preservation and led to competition as well as co-operation with his fellow-men. Secondly, at first man's moral (like his intellectual) powers were of a rudimentary kind; they only gradually developed into the forms we now experience. Lastly, such knowledge (if any) of God as man originally obtained was not immediate and clear; it was always mediated and (as primitive religions still show) distorted in many ways.

All these facts, especially the last, are stressed by Hick. Thus he affirms that 'animal life was first caused to develop into a primitive human consciousness which, so far from being qualified for citizenship in the Kingdom of God, was originally directed towards the absorbing task of mastering a largely hostile environment', and that 'man's spiritual location at an epistemic distance from God makes it virtually inevitable that man will organize his life apart from God and in competition with his fellows'.[5]

Yet I doubt whether this is a complete account of sin's origin. Some forms of moral evil seem to exceed explanation by recourse to the factors I have mentioned. I have in mind unprovoked malice, the pursuit of revenge for its own sake, a senseless and self-destructive desire for power. Also there is cruelty (especially when this takes the form of sheer delight in inflicting pain). We call such sadistic acts 'diabolical' or 'demonic'. And so we approach another account of sin's origin. This is that the human race has been infected by a supernatural power of evil. The place that 'Satan' occupies in Christian thought and the evidence of demonic possession lend support to this view. Yet I see no way of proving it is correct. Also it raises further questions that I find unanswerable. How did evil arise in Satan, and how did he communicate his evil power to mankind? Also a further problem of theodicy would be created by the fact that God permitted human beings to be corrupted by non-human influences over which they have no control.

Next, can we justify the existence of moral evil in a divinely created universe? As I said, I shall first consider the possibility of such a justification solely in terms of this present life and without reference to Christian revelation. The chief argument here is based on the fact of free will and is as follows. If God created us so that we necessarily intended and performed what is right and good we should be mere automata - mere puppets in the hands of the divine puppet-master. The capacity for moral choice belongs to the essence of personality. Hence those who do not possess it are sub-personal, and their relation to God is correspondingly sub-personal.

I do not think that this argument is sound. A being that necessarily did what is right and good need not be a mere puppet or automaton. He would be fully conscious of his acts and their moral value. He could also be fully conscious of God as the source of all good. It is unreasonable to affirm that if the capacity for choice is absent when every other personal property is present the absence of the capacity makes a person less than personal. Furthermore it is possible that angelic beings who are incapable of sin have always existed and employed themselves solely in the praise of God. In any case Christians believe that, by God's grace, the redeemed will achieve a state of indefectible goodness - a *non posse peccare* as against a mere *posse non peccare* - in heaven, and that they will thereby achieve personal fulfilment.

There is, however, an element of truth in the so-called 'free will defence'. A virtue achieved in the face of contrary impulses to which a person might have surrendered differs in kind from a virtue that a person expresses because he is so constituted that he must express it. Moreover it is only an action of which we can say that the agent might have chosen otherwise that is an appropriate object of praise or blame. Hence it can be argued that if it were not for free will a vast area of moral knowledge and experience would be missing. This argument is strengthened by the fact that we often admire most those people who, by self-discipline, have resisted the temptations inherent in their 'lower nature'.

Yet I doubt whether this serves as a complete defence for two reasons. First, according to traditional Christian teaching the area in which free will operates is a comparatively narrow one. We cannot cure ourselves of our sinful tendencies solely of our own volition even if we are sometimes free to resist them. Secondly, there is the harm done to people through the evil choices made by others. Sometimes this harm is irremediable in temporal terms. And so the free will defence needs to be supplemented by an appeal to divine salvation and to the life to come.

What, then, are we to say concerning the origin of non-moral, or physical, evil? I shall dismiss briefly two answers that have been given. First, physical evils have been attributed to man's sin. Admittedly sin has caused some of them (such as some forms of disease). Yet many of them have no connexion with man and have their origins in a pre-human state of the evolutionary process. Secondly, the existence of physical evil may be attributed to the malign influence of supra-human agents. This view will not bear examiniation. If we attribute the creation of the whole physical world to such an agent we shall assign to the latter the creativity due to God alone, and we shall render the benign elements in nature unintelligible. If, however, we attribute to such an agent only those elements in the physical world that are harmful to our species we shall be forced to divide natural processes in a manner that is scientifically untenable. Moreover if it is hard to understand how Satan could influence human beings, it is even harder to understand how a supra-human power could affect nature.

It is obvious that what we call physical evils are for the most part simply the inevitable outcome of the laws that govern the natural world. Thus earthquakes and hurricanes are determined by the state of the earth's substance and by the earth's climatic conditions. Also many, perhaps most, diseases are due to causes of a purely physical kind. Yet this fact prompts the following question. Even if some bodily suffering is inevitable within the structure of our world could not God have modified the structure so that the worst forms of suffering would have been averted? It is very doubtful whether he could have done so. The components of nature are so closely interlocked and in their smallest elements so powerful that even a slight change could cause large-scale effects; so that to ask for even a slight change could entail asking for a very different kind of world. Also although such changes might be welcome in some ways they might be harmful in others.

Speculations concerning what God might have done in order to avert what we call the worst forms of suffering are exposed to two further objections. The first arises from my preceding remarks. Such speculations imply that we are in the position of God, and so are able to examine various ways of creating a world. But of course we are in no such position. Secondly, what do we mean by the 'worst' forms of suffering? It is impossible to enumerate all the forms in such a way that everyone will agree on which forms are worst. Thus toothache, though not lethal, can exceed, in terms of sheer pain, even a mortal illness. Also the capacity to endure pain varies with the sufferer's constitution and circumstances. In any case even if God could have created a world that was free from natural forces that are inherently destructive two forms of physical suffering would remain: the suffering caused by an accidental collision with forces of nature that are inherently beneficent, and suffering inflicted on the sufferer by someone else's sin. God could not prevent the first form without continually performing miracles and so rendering the operations of nature unreliable. He could not prevent the second form without curtailing the moral freedom of those who perform the sinful acts that cause harm to others.

Can we, then, justify problematic cases of suffering in purely temporal terms? It has been held that we can do on the grounds, first that suffering benefits the sufferer, and secondly that it also benefits others. Certainly suffering can be beneficial in both these ways. It can increase or induce virtues (such as gentleness and patience) in the sufferer. Also the example of suffering nobly borne can inspire others and elicit from them a compassion that would not otherwise be shown. Yet suffering is not invariably beneficial. Sometimes it overwhelms the sufferer and makes him incapable of a moral response. Sometimes too it is not noticed by others so that it cannot be of any service to them. In short, some unmerited suffering (often of an acute and prolonged kind) is, if judged in terms of this life only, apparently pointless.

I therefore conclude that there is no completely adequate answer to either of the following questions (when they are raised in a theistic context): (a) how did evil originate? and (b) can it be justified in terms of this world only and without any reference to Christ? And so I pass to (c) - to a scrutiny of evil's cure considered in terms of the life to come and Christian revelation.

The question of moral evil's cure leads immediately to the doctrine of Atonement with which I shall deal separately in the next chapter. The essence of the doctrine can be simply summarized. Christ, as the incarnate Word, offers to all men a power by which they can be freed from sin, reconciled to God, and achieve the spiritual perfection that he intends for them. Certainly they (or at any rate most of them) achieve this partially and intermittently in this life; but they will achieve it fully and continuously in the life to come.

Deferring then for the moment the question of sin I shall consider the question of suffering. The traditional answer given by many theists is that the sufferings of this life will be remedied by eternal joy in the life to come. This answer is stated thus by Paul: 'I consider that the sufferings of this present time are not worth comparing with the glory that is to be revealed in us'.[6] The strength of the answer depends upon our interpretation of the joy by which suffering will ultimately be compensated. If it is to be a merely human joy it may not seem to counter-balance and so to rectify the worst suffering that has been endured. However, according to the Christian hope that Paul expresses the joy will not be merely human; it will be divine. It will consist in the vision of God. Moreover, the soul will not see God only as the self-existent and glorious Creator. It will see him also as the One who loves all his spiritual creatures infinitely, who sympathizes with them in all their afflictions, and who offers them nothing less than the eternal happiness that comes from fellowship with him.

There is, however, an objection that must be met at this point. It is sometimes claimed that not even eternal joy would rectify innocent suffering that was of no benefit to the sufferer and that therefore did not function as a means of growth towards spiritual perfection. The injustice and pointlessness of such suffering would remain; and nothing could expunge them. Although I feel the force of this objection, especially when I relate it to cases within my own experience, I believe it can be answered as follows. There are two reasons for holding that God could not apportion suffering so that it would always benefit the sufferer. I have mentioned both in the context of a closely connected, but different, question. If God were to apportion suffering thus he would need to be constantly performing miracles (where the maleficent forces of nature are concerned) or to be constantly obstructing human freedom (where maleficent acts of will are concerned). In an ordered world that leaves room for free choice it is inevitable that some forms of suffering should not be beneficial. Of course those who are overwhelmed by suffering from which there is no escape cannot now recognize this fact. Yet they will recognize it hereafter. And the recognition of it, when taken together with their vision of God's love, will vindicate his justice in their sight.

Yet the Christian hope consists in more even than this. The 'glory' of which Paul spoke is the 'glory of God in the face of Christ'.[7] Even in this life Christ, as the incarnate Son of God, constitutes an answer to the problem of suffering in three ways.

1. Christ imparts a new significance to the vicarious quality of suffering. As the suffering Servant of the Lord predicted in Isaiah 53 he is the supreme and unsurpassable instance of the way in which unmerited suffering, when endured in faith and love, can bring salvation to others. His disciples who imitate him by the aid of his Spirit can have the same effect on others. One thinks chiefly of the early Christian martyrs who have brought spiritual strength to so many

people by their heroism. The same effect has been achieved by countless Christians who, though not officially ranked as martyrs or saints, have met pain, desolation and misunderstanding after the example of their Lord.

2. If God suffered for us in Christ's humanity in a manner that was wholly undeserved and designed wholly for our good we have no right to complain if we also suffer undeservedly. A true contemplation of the Cross removes resentment. The most compelling statement of this truth known to me occurs towards the end of A. J. Balfour's Gifford Lectures:[8]

> 'What is needed is such a living faith in God's relation to Man as shall leave no place for that helpless resentment against the appointed Order so apt to rise within us at the sight of undeserved pain. And this faith is possessed by those who vividly realise the Christian form of theism. For they worship One Who is no remote contriver of a universe to whose ills He is indifferent. If they suffer, did He not on their account suffer also? If suffering falls not always on the most guilty, was He not innocent? Shall they cry aloud that the world is ill-designed for their convenience, when He for their sakes subjected Himself to its conditions? It is true that beliefs like these do not in any narrow sense resolve our doubts nor provide us with explanations. But they give us something better than many explanations. For they minister, or rather the Reality behind them ministers, to one of our deepest ethical needs: to a need which, far from showing signs of diminution, seems to grow with the growth of civilisation, and to touch us ever more keenly as the hardness of an earlier time dissolves away.'

3. Christians do not merely imitate Christ's sufferings and respond to the divine love that the sufferings revealed. They are actually united with Christ's sufferings in a manner that contributes both to their own redemtpion and to the redemption of other people. Of course this union does not enable us to repeat Christ's sufferings that are unique both in themselves and in their salvific power. Nevertheless the union enables Christians to turn their sufferings, as Christ turned his, into occasions for offering themselves anew to God in obedience, trust and love. One test of sanctification is the extent to which the believer is able to make fruitful use of his unmerited suffering through submission to, and transformation by, the Spirit of Christ.

However, two qualifications are required. First, the same limitations that affect a generally theistic interpretation of suffering also affect Christian theodicy. Much suffering on the part of Christians, as of non-Christians, passes unobserved and is not of any benefit to others. Also some suffering undergone by Christians, as by non-Christians, deprives them at the time of a capacity for a spiritual response. Secondly, we have to take account of those who, through no fault of their own, do not believe in Christ.

Hence we must postulate immortality for the fulfilment of the cure Christ offers for innocent suffering. This appeal to a future life is based firmly on the New Testament. Even to Christ the divine significance of his sufferings was not apparent before his death. On the contrary he prayed that he might be spared the Cross, and when he was crucified he felt himself to be forsaken by God. He was not vindicated until the Resurrection. Hence it is only in the next life that, through union with Christ, each sufferer will 'see the fruit of the travail of his soul and be satisfied'.[9] When Paul said that we suffer with Christ that we may be glorified with him[10] he meant the glory reserved for us in the life to come. In that life all innocent sufferers will find their sufferings transfigured by union with Christ's sufferings and by participation in the glory that these sufferings produced. No innocent suffering will be merely ours. It will be ours only 'in Christ' in relation to his role as the one in whom the whole meaning of history will be summed up. Even suffering that was (or at any rate seemed to be) pointless on earth will achieve significance when it is united with Christ's sufferings; for such sufferers will then be able to offer their sufferings with the sacrificed life that Christ presents to the Father on our behalf; and through this self-offering their sufferings will be transfigured both by the redemptive meaning of Christ's sacrifice and by the glorification of his sacrifice in his exalted state.

I must leave a full inquiry into the theme of union with Christ until the next chapter. Meanwhile there is a further difficulty I must mention. It is one that preachers and apologists sometimes evade. The arguments I have presented presuppose that in the life to come sufferers will be capable of responding fully to God and to Christ as his incarnation. What, then, are we to say of young children and imbeciles who die without a capacity for this response? I do not know of any answer to this question which is, to my mind, the most perplexing in theodicy.

Before I turn to the final question of evil's justification in terms of its divine cure there is a basic difficulty with which I must deal. I have been forced to admit areas in which evil evades rational explanation. Thus I have admitted that the origin of moral evil in its extreme forms is not fully explicable. I have also admitted that we are unable to envisage how even a supernatural cure of evil can affect those who die with their rational powers undeveloped or congenitally impaired. To an atheist or agnostic these admissions are bound to seem damaging. But to a Christian, or even perhaps to a non-Christian theist who is prepared to consider sympathetically the claims of Christianity, I suggest that they are acceptable on the following grounds.

(i) We are compelled to be ignorant of many things in theology. The closest parallel lies in the domain of eschatology. As I shall show, in my view we are forced to be agnostic concerning the answers given to many questions we naturally ask about the life to come. The parallel is made especially relevant by the fact that apart from belief in immortality the problem of evil cannot be finally solved.

(ii) In the sphere of theodicy we possess considerable knowledge. Thus the origin of sin is largely intelligible. Also we can see a partial justification of sin and suffering even in terms of this world.

Furthermore in almost all cases we can understand in principle that the incarnate and risen Christ is a final cure of evil. Even when we are forced to be agnostic concerning the destiny of infants and imbeciles we can adopt the attitude commended thus by A. M. Farrer. 'We do not know where to draw the line; that is to say, we do not know where God draws it. But we may be sure that he loves and saves whatever is there to be saved or loved; if his love or power does not act it is because there is nothing for it to act upon.'[11]

(iii) As the book of Job dramatically shows, an inability to explain suffering can serve two purposes. It can act as a 'trial' of faith, an element in faith's 'probation' of which the author of 1 Peter wrote as follows at the beginning of his epistle: 'In this you rejoice, though now for a little while you may have to suffer various trials, so that the genuineness of your faith, more precious than gold which though perishable is tested by fire, may redound to praise and honour at the revelation of Jesus Christ'.[12] The second use of inexplicable suffering is to increase our sense of God's mystery as the one whose nature and ways surpass man's understanding.

I come now to my final question (d). Does God's cure of evil in terms of the Incarnation and immortality justify the existence of evil in a world that he has created? Manifestly it does so in so far as the cure totally annuls or transfigures the evil. Moreover the good inherent in the cure totally transcends all evil in so far as, while evil is natural and temporal, the good is supernatural and eternal. Yet would it not have been still better if God had created a world in which there was no evil but through which, nevertheless, men could achieve eternal communion with him? This question is bound to seem improper to a theist who disclaims any *a priori* knowledge of God's mind, and who is committed to the belief that whatever God does is an inevitable expression of his love. Yet even from our human standpoint the question can be answered in two ways.

First, God may have created another world or other worlds in which evil cannot arise. But in the world we inhabit it was either certain or probable that evil would arise. Hence to ask that God should have created a world in which evil could not occur is to ask for a world that is essentially different from the one we inhabit. Yet to ask for a different kind of world is self-stultifying. To imagine that it would have been better if God had not created our world is to imagine that it would have been better if we did not exist. Here we easily commit the fallacy of thinking that we could be the same beings even if we existed in another world. But our personal identities are inseparable from our heredity and environment. I would not be 'I' apart from innumerable factors in my past and my present. And all these factors are conditioned by the unique, unrepeatable, world I inhabit.

Secondly, although God is not obliged by any kind of external constraint to create every kind of world or even one kind rather than another we can see a sign of his wisdom in the fact (if it is a fact) that he has chosen to create different kinds of worlds containing spiritual creatures; for each kind can contribute towards an ultimate and total Good. Let us suppose that there are discarnate intelligences who have never known evil. At 'the end' when God shall be 'all in all' they will constitute one form of good. Human creatures who have been redeemed from evil will constitute another form of good. Both forms will be special, non-substitutable, reflections of God's glory. Each form too will enrich the other by a mutual sharing of experiences.

Finally, so far as belief in the Incarnation is concerned the following facts must constantly be borne in mind.

1. For bare theism of a kind that Christians share with Jews and Muslims evil arises as a secondary problem that then inevitably prompts the questions I have raised. Starting with belief in an omnipotent and all-loving Creator we ask how belief can be reconciled with the fact of evil. We are then impelled to speculate concerning the possibility of a necessarily perfect world. However, as Christians we do not know God apart from evil. We know him only as our Saviour from it. Hence to demand a justification of evil is tantamount to demanding a justification of Christianity. That is why Christians have been continually driven to endorse the ancient paradox: *O felix culpa quae talem ac tantum meruit habere Redemptorem* (O happy guilt that deserved to have so good and so great a Redeemer). And what applies to guilt applies, in the light of Christ's passion, to innocent suffering also.

2. The fact of evil has often been regarded as being incompatible with belief in God's love. The *prima facie* incompatibility is obvious. Yet the paradox I have mentioned here has its maximum degree of applicability. Love at its best includes a desire on the part of the lover to give himself as far as possible to, and to identify himself as far as possible with, the person loved. And not even God could reveal his infinite love as effectively as he did by giving himself to sinful men and sharing their pains. Of couse nothing human can add to or subtract from God's love *per se*. Yet human evil prompted the greatest possible expression of his love.

3. The Incarnation solves the problem created by the fact that God is responsible for evil in the sense that he created a world in which it was either certain (in the case of suffering) or probable (in the case of sin) that evil would arise. I do not think it is too much to say that by becoming man God acknowledged this responsibility. At the same time he justified himself by revealing the full extent of his love for his human creatures and by enabling them to acquire a supernatural mode of being through participation in the humanity he assumed.

There is one further concept that, because of its historical importance, I must mention. Many theologians have defined evil as a 'privation of good' (*privatio boni*). This is manifestly not a complete definition. In itself it could suggest that evil is merely negative or even unreal. But evil is a positive force and it possesses its own, horrifying, reality. However, it is at the same time a privation of good in both the moral and the teleological senses of the word; it signifies the absence of some entity, property or state that is morally desirable and that contributes towards the fulfilment of a person or persons. Here are two examples from the spheres of non-moral and moral evil respectively. While blindness is positive and real it is also a privation of sight. Again while cruelty is positive and real both *per se* and in its effects it is also a privation of love.

Moreover, there are four reasons for affirming that evil is a *privatio boni.*

First, evil takes its whole meaning from good. As Aquinas put it, 'evil cannot be known simply as evil, for its core is hollow, and can be neither recognized nor defined save by the surrounding good'.[13] Thus to call 'blindness' and 'cruelty' evil implies a reference to 'sight' and 'love'. Evil is always conceptually parasitical on the good to which it is opposed. Hence it is always known in terms of this oppostion.

Secondly, this conceptual fact reflects the ontological fact that evil, though real, does not exist as an independent power. Cosmic dualism is thereby excluded. Once again, the doctrine of creation has primacy. All theists believe that the world was created *ex nihilo* by a God of love. Christians believe that the Creator's love was decisively revealed in Christ. Hence evil can exist only as something that God permits as a means for achieving the ultimate good that he intends for all his creatures.

Thirdly, because moral evil is a privation of the good (in both the moral and the teleological senses of the word) that God intends for his human creatures it is bound, ultimately, to deceive the evil person and destroy him. The supreme example of such self-deception and self-destruction in this century was Hitler. Having devoted himself as the leader of his nation to the pursuit of diabolical evil he inevitably ended by committing suicide after deluding himself that he could still win the war he had caused. And so he epitomized hell on earth.

Lastly, because evil is not an autonomous power, and because it contains the seeds of its self-destruction, it cannot permanently survive in a world created by a God of love. God is bound to defeat it in the end, in his own manner and in his own time. This much can be affirmed by all theists. Christian theists further believe that they have a supernaturally effective symbol of God's victory in the life, death and resurrection of his incarnate Son.

These, then, in my view are the basic principles of Christian theodicy. However, it is one thing to give answers (in so far as these are available) to the problem of evil; but it is another thing to endure evil when it affects oneself or those whom one loves. How far the evidence and arguments I have given will comfort and sustain Christians in distress is hard to estimate. I should certainly not expect them to be sufficient in all circumstances. From a practical point of view four further things must be said.

1. We must try to distinguish between those evils that we can and those that we cannot remedy. At first sight this may seem to be a merely prudential maxim. Yet it is also part of a religious attitude in so far as it rests on the recogntion that although God has left some evils under our control he has reserved others for a remedy that we are unable to effect. Hence with regard to the latter evils we must resign ourselves to his providence. Nevertheless such resignation is not distinctively Christian. It was advocated by the Stoics. And so it needs to be strengthened by other facts.

2. The chief fact is that of Christ's passion. I have already stated the significance of the Cross for theodicy. Yet it is possible to give notional assent to the redemptive power of Christ's sacrifice without giving it real assent. To give it real assent means to experience its reality here and now as a transfiguring power in one's own existence. This experience cannot be obtained in a moment as a sudden relief from sin or suffering. Paul made it the aim of his whole life to be conformed to the pattern of Christ's death and resurrection. The Resurrection is the ground of the third fact.

3. The Christian is called on to cultivate a sense of immortality. He must consistently see this life in the light of the life to come. Yet this vision must be christo-centric. The eternal life for which he hopes is the life won for him by the risen Christ. And just as we cannot experience the transforming power of the Cross in some evil that suddenly engulfs us unless we experience it in our lives as a whole, so we cannot experience the transforming power of the Resurrection in the midst of unexpected evil unless we view all events *sub specie eternitatis*

4. The Christian must always remember that in facing evil he is not alone. Other Christians have both endured and witnessed the worst forms of suffering without bitterness or loss of faith. Through their union with the crucified and risen Christ they have continually used suffering in order to increase their self-surrender to God and their awareness of his presence. Thereby they have obtained a serenity and joy that have both astonished and inspired those who have known them. This inspiration is part of what is meant by 'the communion of saints'.

There are two other forms of evil of which I have not so far spoken but on which I must comment from a practical point of view. The first form consists in the feeling, experienced by most people at some time, that life is meaningless. That this feeling is evil is surely obvious. It is spiritually ennervating; it can blind us to what is good; and at its worst it can produce despair. Secondly, there is the feeling that God is absent from the world of our experience. This feeling is especially painful if it is contrasted with previous moments when God seemed intensely real and near. Sometimes these feelings are caused by our sin. We have not persevered in prayer or availed ourselves of the manifold help that the Church provides. At other times they occur through no apparent fault of our own. When they thus occur we must recollect the factors I have mentioned with reference to the endurance of sin and suffering.

Primarily there is the fact of Christ. Even he experienced frustration and was unable, in his human consciousness, to perceive the outcome of his ministry. Moreover, even he felt himself to be deserted by God in his passion. Next, there is the eschatological perspective. In the purpose of God the final meaning of our lives rests, not in this world, but in the world to come, when all things will be fulfilled in Christ. Lastly, many Christians of unquestioned holiness have been called on to endure periods of spiritual aridity in which God seems absent and in which they have adhered to him by a pure act of faith.

I claim only to have stated the basis of the Christian answer to the problem constituted by the existence of evil in a world created by an omnipotent God of love. What I have said needs to be supplemented in two ways. First, I have concentrated on the question raised by the fact of innocent suffering. I have given no more than a summary of the Christian answer to the question of moral evil (or sin). Yet from a Christian standpoint salvation consists primarily in deliverance from sin and, as a consequence, from the suffering that sin entails. Secondly, I have affirmed that the Christian answer to the question raised by innocent suffering consists in union with the incarnate and risen Christ. But I have not so far explained the nature of the union. I shall complete my discussion of evil on both these points in the following two chapters.

[1] *Evil and the God of Love* (London 1966, p 75).
[2] Op. cit., pp 196-7.
[3] *Nature, Man and God* (London 1935, p 366).
[4] Op. cit., p 370.
[5] Op cit., pp 321-22.
[6] Rom. 8. 18.
[7] 2 Cor. 4. 6.
[8] *The Foundations of Belief* (London 1895, p 354).
[9] Is. 53. 11.
[10] Rom. 8. 17.
[11] *Love Almighty and Ills Unlimited (London 1962, p 190)*.
[12] 1 Pet 1. 6-7.
[13] S.T. 1a. XIV. 10. (Taken from Gilby's *Philosophical Texts*, Oxford 1956, p 163).

CHAPTER 6
CHRIST THE SAVIOUR

I have already dealt in part with this theme in discussing the ways in which Christ can be regarded as the cure of non-moral evil or suffering. In this chapter I shall consider him as the Saviour from moral evil or sin. From the beginning Christianity has been a Gospel (good news) of deliverance from sin through the life, death and resurrection of Christ. To express the fact of this deliverance theologians have used other words besides salvation. Chief among these are redemption, reconciliation and atonement. Yet salvation is the most inclusive word, just as it is the one that has been most widely used.

A few preliminary remarks on these other words are necessary. 'To redeem' means literally 'to buy back or recover'. This implies that men are in a thraldom to sin from which Christ rescues them by the 'price' of his death. 'Reconciliation' implies that men, through their sin, are at enmity with God and that Christ converts them from being God's enemies to being his friends. 'Atonement', if taken in its literal sense as at-one-ment is equivalent to 'reconciliation'; but it has come to signify the means by which reconciliation is effected. All these words, therefore, signify various aspects of salvation.

From the beginning too Christians have claimed that Christ is the *sole* mediator of salvation. Thus Peter is represented as saying that 'there is salvation in no one else, for there is no other name under heaven given among men by which we must be saved'.[1] Again the fourth evangelist attributes to Christ the words: 'I am the way, and the truth and the life; no one comes to the Father, but by me'.[2] In the same vein Paul claims that only by Christ can we be justified (that is, restored to a right relationship with God), and the author of the epistle to the Hebrews affirms that Christ's sacrifice is our only means of access to the heavenly world.

Some Christians have attempted to combine these claims for Christ as the Saviour with the view that he was merely human. In the second chapter I gave reasons for holding that this attempt is bound to fail. Unless Christ was God incarnate we cannot validly affirm that he is unequalled, unsurpassable and indispensable as the mediator of salvation. Belief in the absolute uniqueness and finality of his work implies belief in the absolute uniqueness and finality of his person. In any case (as a matter of historical fact) the Fathers always interpreted the Atonement in the light of the Incarnation. Hence I shall presuppose the doctrine of the Incarnation in all that follows.

Various accounts have been given of the ways in which Christ effects our salvation. I suggest that from a study of the New Testament four main ways emerge.

1. The Incarnation is a unique revelation of God's love. 'God so loved the world that he gave his only Son that whoever believes in him should not perish but have eternal life.'[3] Again, God shows his love for us in that while we were yet sinners Christ died for us'.[4] The contemplation of this love is salvific in two ways. By revealing the full extent of our self-centredness it awakens in us true penitence. Furthermore it demands from us a reciprocal love towards God and a consequent surrender of our lives to him. The first of these ways was stated by Augustine thus. 'This we do well to believe, indeed to hold fixed and immovable in our hearts, that the humility which God displayed in being born of a woman and in being haled so ignominiously by mortal men to death, is the sovereign medicine for healing our swollen pride, the profound mystery by which the bond of sin is broken.'[5] The second way is expressed as follows in a stanza of a well-known hymn. 'Were the whole realm of nature mine, that were an offering far too small; love so amazing, so divine, demands my soul, my life, my all.'

2. Christ by his life and death gave us a perfect example of obedience to God and so restored the divine image that sin had defaced. Admittedly the New Testament sometimes states this truth in terms that many people today find unacceptable or alien. Thus Paul describes Christ's obedience by contrast with the disobedience of a first man, Adam. Again, the author of the epistle to the Hebrews describes it by contrast with the sacrifices of Judaism. However, the truth remains even if these contrasts are rejected. God requires of his human creatures a perfect obedience to his will. In other words, he requires of them an absolute self-sacrifice motivated by love for him and for their fellow-creatures. Yet because of the sin by which they are both individually and corporately afflicted they cannot offer this obedience. Christ offers it as their representative, and so he becomes the founder of a 'new creation', 'the first-born among many brethren'.

3. Yet according to the New Testament we are not called merely to imitate Christ's obedience from afar. Christ is not only external to us; he also lives within us by his risen power. 'It is no longer I who live', says Paul, 'but Christ who lives in me; and the life I now live in the flesh I live by faith in the Son of God who loved me and gave himself for me'.[6] The fourth evangelist speaks likewise. Christ is the vine; disciples are the branches. They dwell in him, and he dwells in them. Together (in Paul's language again) they constitute a Body of which he is the head. He is omnipresent among those who believe in him and love him, bestowing on them his own risen life.

4. Christ defeated evil in all its forms. This is the so-called *Christus Victor* motiv that Gustav Aulen regarded as the classical theory of the Atonement. The truth in this theory is double. First, by his death and resurrection Christ overcame all the forces of evil that had crucified him. Secondly, he overcomes the evil that infects our own natures. He does so in the ways I have just stated - by revealing his Father's love, by offering an example of perfect obedience, and by enabling us to share

in the victory he won on our behalf. The New Testament also states that Christ conquered Satan and the cosmic powers of evil. This immediately raises the question whether Satan and his minions exist. I myself remain agnostic on the point. But if Satan does exist we must surely take the affirmation of Christ's victory over him to mean that Christ delivers men from his dominion and so deprives him of his *raison d'être*. The view (held by some of the Fathers) that Christ delivered men by paying Satan a ransom or by ensnaring him is singularly unconvincing and is not, I assume, likely to be held by any of my readers.

Other views of the Atonement have been proposed. Thus (to take the main examples) theologians have held that Christ's death was necessary to propitiate God's anger; that it was an act of satisfaction offered to God's honour that sinners have insulted and to which they are in debt; that it was a substitutionary sacrifice whereby Christ paid on our behalf the penalty that our sin has incurred. I maintain that the first view is wholly false and that although the second and third views contain elements of truth they are false in the forms I have stated.

The first view depends on the concept of God's anger or wrath. Whether wrath is attributable to God at all, even by analogy, is doubtful. However, if we do attribute it to him we can mean one of two things. We can mean that God is angry because sinners have offended his person; or we can take his anger to mean the 'righteous indignation' that he, as the holy one, feels when he contemplates sin and its effects. The first of these meanings is both religiously and morally reprehensible. It represents God as being actuated by an injured self-esteem that would be regarded as a defect even in an earthly king; and it is inconsistent with the belief that God is infinite in generosity towards his creatures. The further idea that the Father would allow his self-esteem to be appeased by the innocent sacrifice of his Son is even more reprehensible and is also inconsistent with the belief that the Son is the uncreated object of his love. The second meaning of 'wrath' is more acceptable. Yet if we say that God's holiness causes him to be angry at the sight of sin we cannot validly affirm that Christ's death appeased his anger. If he is angry, his anger, because it proceeds from pure love, ceases as soon as sin is removed. Christ would then indirectly cause God's anger to cease by delivering us from sin; but he would not directly cause it to cease by appeasing it.

The elements of truth in the second view (first propounded by Anselm) are that our obedience to God is his 'due' (or, alternatively, that it is our duty to obey him); that sin therefore puts us in his debt; and that Christ, as the perfect man, rendered to him the perfect obedience that we have failed to render. Yet the view is vitiated by two errors. First, God does not demand payment of the debt that is owing to him in order to satisfy his wounded honour. To postulate this demand is to represent him, not as a loving Father, but as a feudal lord. Secondly, Christ's obedience is not a substitute for ours as a means of paying the debt that our disobedience has incurred. Rather it is an example that we are to follow through the power of his Spirit.

The truth in the third view is that Christ's death was the penalty he paid for fulfilling the Messianic task that God had set for him. 'The Son of Man must suffer.' This dominical saying must be taken in its historical context to mean that if Jesus was to reveal the Father's love and be obedient to the Father's will he was bound to end his days on a cross. Here I agree with these words written by Dom Illtyd Trethowan. 'Christ suffered and died because of our sins in that this was the consequence of his living a perfect, fully human, life in the circumstances of the world-order which sin had brought about. This is the price which he had to pay for living among us.'[7] Yet Jesus did not pay in our stead a penalty that our sins have incurred. Rather, by his sacrifice on our behalf he delivered us from both sin and its penalty.

My reasons for rejecting these three theories of the Atonement can be summed up under three heads.

1. They all imply that Christ's death was necessary in order to make our reconciliation with God possible. God's honour must be satisfied, his wrath appeased, his ordained penalty for sin be paid. Yet this implication is wholly incompatible with the idea of forgiveness. And God's forgiveness of our sins is a primary, ineradicable, datum of the gospel. This incompatibility can be shown by a human analogy. If A has sinned against his friend B then B can adopt one of two courses. He can either forgive A freely or he can demand a recompense or penalty from A; but he cannot do both simultaneously. Surely no one would dream of saying to a friend who has injured him; 'I forgive you on the condition that you render satisfaction or pay a penalty for the wrong you have done me'. Forgiveness is by its nature unconditional.

2. The New Testament throughout affirms that God's forgiveness is unconditional. Thus Jesus taught his disciples to pray simply 'forgive us our debts'. And he himself forgave sins on his own authority. Although he refers to his death as a means of redemption he nowhere implies that it is a necessary condition of God's forgiveness. Paul rules out the idea of such a necessity in many ways. Chiefly he insists that we are saved by grace alone, and that God's righteousness is revealed, not in a demand for satisfaction or for a penalty, but in his free acquittal of sinners and in his unmerited restoration of them to communion with himself. The matter is summed up thus by Vincent Taylor. 'The New Testament does not teach that Christ died in order that God might be able to forgive sins. The remission of sins is an act of God's free grace, whereby, in response to the cry of the contrite, he sets aside the barriers raised by our sins and makes possible our reconciliation to himself.'[8]

3. The theories of satisfaction and penal substitution confuse moral and legal categories. In the legal sphere a debt must be paid and a penalty discharged. However, there is no such necessity in the moral sphere. On the contrary, a loving father will readily waive a debt owed to him by his own son, just as he will do all he can to save his son from the self-destructive effects that his son's sins have caused. Moreover,

although in the legal sphere one person can sometimes pay a debt or penalty owed by another, in the moral sphere he cannot do so. Moral responsibility is incommunicable.

Christ, then, did not die in order to remove, by a substitutionary sacrifice, an obstacle that God had placed in the way of forgiveness. God is always ready to forgive sinners on the sole conditions that they repent and show towards their fellow men the same mercy that they expect from him. The relation between divine forgiveness and Christ's death is threefold. First, the Cross, when seen as the self-sacrifice of God incarnate, is the supreme revelation of the love from which God's forgiveness proceeds. Secondly (as the words of Augustine I quoted indicate) because it is such a revelation it supremely possesses the capacity to awaken in us the repentance without which God's forgiveness cannot be received. Thirdly, forgiveness is not only negative and retrospective; it is also positive and prospective. It is negative and retrospective in so far as it is an act by which God, through a pure exercise of pardon, blots out our sins and resolves not to hold them against us. But it is also positive and prospective in so far as by it God confers on forgiven sinners a new relation with himself. To say that we are forgiven through the Cross is to say that God confers on us a share in the new relation with him that Christ fulfilled by his final sacrifice. Correspondingly, from a Christian standpoint, true repentance means a readiness to identify oneself with Christ in his death to sin and in his self-offering to God. The theme of identification with Christ brings me to a final observation on the theories of atonement I have criticized.

Even if these theories were wholly true they would be defective is isolating the Cross from the Resurrection, and so in removing Christ's saving work from any immediate relation to the believer. The most they do is to state the means of atonement. They do not state its goal. The goal is union with Christ. Even if Christ did satisfy divine justice, propitiate divine wrath, and pay sin's penalty, these acts would be only means towards union with him in his exalted state. Within the New Testament this union is definitively affirmed by the fourth evangelist who thereby places the Atonement firmly in the setting of the Incarnation and the Trinity. The Word became flesh, he tells us, in order that by the Holy Spirit, the Paraclete, we might be united with him in his union with the Father. This view of the Atonement has been constantly expressed by subsequent theologians. Yet it has been characteristic of the Eastern rather than the Western church. Forensic interpretations of the Atonement have always been more emphasized in the Latin West than in the Greek East. This is how John Meyendorf sums up the Eastern view: 'In Greek patristic and Byzantine thought salvation is understood essentially in terms of participation in and communion with the deified humanity of the incarnate Logos, the new Adam'.[9]

I maintain, then, that the essence of the Atonement is composed of the four elements in the New Testament's teaching that I stated at the beginning of this chapter. The ground of the Atonement consists in, first, God's great act of love in becoming man for our salvation, and secondly in Christ's life of perfect obedience. The goal of the Atonement consists in union with the victorious Christ through the indwelling power of the Holy Spirit. All elements of truth that are contained in other theories of the Atonement are included within these Biblical affirmations.

Finally, union with Christ is supernatural in two respects. First, in so far as it is constituted by God's supernatural revelation in Christ it exceeds any communion with God that we are able to achieve solely by our created powers. Secondly, through this union Christ communicates to us the life of his own glorified humanity and so enables us to share in his filial relation to the Father. Here we must avoid the followng extremes. On the one hand we must not affirm that Christians are actually deified. The ontological distinction between the Creator and all creatures is absolute and permanent. Also to affirm that Christians receive a portion of the Godhead would be incompatible with the fact that even in the hypostatic union the divine and human natures were not fused. We cannot receive a portion even of Christ's humanity or reduplicate its divine functions. On the other hand it is insufficeint to interpret Christ's relation to us solely in terms of the external influence that one human person can exert on another. Those scriptural passages that speak of Christ's indwelling power must be given their full force. Christ is really present in disciples through the Holy Spirit; he really communicates his risen life to them; he really re-creates them in his image.

A specially profound discussion of union with Chirst is contained in Emile Mersch's *The Theology of the Mystical Body.*[10] Mersch sums up the matter thus. 'In Christ and in the new union that is given to mankind in him, a new way of existing is inaugurated. A new way of existing that is supernatural. Fully realized in Christ, it spreads from him over the whole vastness of his mystical body; and this is the mystery of the Church. Through the Church it flows into each soul; and this is the mystery of grace.'[11] Christ does not change the nature of the person whom he indwells by adding some new property or quality. 'The supernatural involves a change of a different order, a change that is at once far more radical and more delicate, a change that affects a being by causing it to be the very thing it was but in a different way.'[12] Mersch then restates this truth by contrasting God's act of creation with his act of re-creation. 'When God has communicated himself to a thing by the being that is interior to the thing, he can still communicate himself by the being that is interior to himself. The resulting enhancement will be less an addition of being than a deepening and an interiorization of the being that was already there. As first cause, God has already acted on the thing by causing it to exist; now he acts by uniting his own perfect being with the being of the thing, thereby causing it to exist in a more perfect way.'[13]

As the language used by Mersch indicates, the supernaturalization of the creature by Christ, being wholly unique, cannot be explained in other terms. Just as God's first act of creation is *sui generis* so also is his second act in re-creating us in the image of his incarnate Son. His second act is even less amenable to our understanding than his first. We can form some analogies for his first act in terms of our own creative powers. But we cannot form any analogies for the second. God's act in communicating to us his own nature through the human nature he assumed is bound to exceed our comprehension. We can experience it; we can discern its fruits in lives of Christian sanctity; but we cannot even begin to comprehend its *modus operandi*.

I shall now consider three questions that the Christian concept of atonement raises. I suggest that all of them must be finally answered in terms of the view that the goal of atonement consists in union with God incarnate.

1. The Gospel presupposes that all men are sinners who, on account of their sin, are in need of divine salvation. Yet can the truth of this presupposition be proved? I do not think it is possible to produce a complete proof that will convince believers and unbelievers equally. The concept of sin is a complex one that can be analysed in various ways. For my present purpose it is enough to make two distinctions. The first is between the religious and the purely ethical senses of sin. According to the first sense sin is disobedience to God's will and a rejection of his love. According to the second sense it is a failure to achieve those ideals of rightness and goodness that we perceive in purely moral terms. The two senses are closely connected. If God is the source of goodness a failure to love him is bound to be a moral failure as well as a religious one. Conversely all evil acts offend God. As the greatest of the penitential Psalms puts it, 'Against thee have I sinned, against thee only have I sinned and done this evil in thy sight'.[14] The second distinction is between original sin (consisting in sinful impulses that all men possess) and actual sin (consisting in sinful acts that men commit of their own free choice).

As I have said, I do not think it is possible to prove beyond all doubt that all men are sinners in both the preceding ways. Some theologians have attempted to prove it by affirming a 'seminal identity' of all mankind with Adam. I have already rejected the view that sin originated with Adam's fall; and the whole idea of such an identity strikes me as being spiritually meaningless. *A fortiori* we cannot prove that all men are so sinful that they can be delivered from their sin only by a supernatural act of redemption. Nevertheless, if we assume that sin entered the world, not through one man, but throughout the human race when men first evolved from their pre-human past, we can reasonably assume also that sinful tendencies would have spread and increased by both imitation and reaction. Yet we are not left with mere hypotheses. All the evidence based on both recorded history and present observation indicates that sin in both its original and its actual

forms has been and still is unversal, if not in the strict sense of being
present in every man, at least in the broader sense of being present in
every type of man and every type of society. The same evidence shows
conclusively that in every aspect of human existence the corrupting
and destructive power of sin is incalculable. Sin, moreover, often
corrupts or destroys, not only the sinner, but also others who bear no
responsibility for his sin. One of the most distressing problems in
theodicy is the harm inflicted by the wicked on the innocent. I am not
suggesting that all men are totally depraved. On the contrary it seems
to me clear that 'fallen' man retains good impulses and the capacity to
choose the good in the face of contrary inclinations. The divine image
in man has been scarred, but not destroyed. Yet the facts fully support
the view that it has been scarred beyond the point at which it can be
humanly cured.

We must reckon with two further facts. First, from a theistic
standpoint even a morally blameless person would be radically
imperfect if he did not direct his life out of a conscious love for God; so
that he would still need conversion. Secondly, there is the fact of
Christian experience. And this fact is bound to be determinative for
Christian belief. Christians have constantly felt themselves to belong
to a spiritually perverted race even when they have rejected a literalistic
understanding of Adam's fall. A personal sense of sin and a personal
conviction that Christ is the only means of redemption pervade the
New Testament; they are embedded in the Church's liturgy; and they
are echoed in the experience of all the Church's saints and mystics..
Without them Christianity is unintelligible.

However let us suppose - and it is a supposition for which I have no
evidence - that there exists a person who is sinless or whose sins are of a
purely venial kind. Let us further suppose that his life is dominated by
love for God so that he is fit for communion with him. Let us further
suppose that he does not suffer through the sins of others. He would
still lack the supernatural perfection that union with Christ bestows.
Moreover in order to obtain that perfection he would need to
participate imaginatively in the experience of those who have obtained
it by redemption from sin and reliance on Christ as the divine
Redeemer.

2. There is the question whether the Incarnation is the only means of
salvation that God could have adopted. Some theologians have
answered this question affirmatively. Thus Athanasius wrote as
follows:[15]

> 'We have, then, now stated in part, as far as it was possible, and as
> ourselves had been able to understand, the reason of his bodily
> appearing; that it was in the power of none other to turn the corruptible
> to incorruption, except the Saviour himself, that had at the beginning
> also made all things out of nought; and that none other could create
> anew the likeness of God's image for men, save the image of the Father;
> and that none other could render the mortal immortal, save our Lord
> Jesus Christ, who is the very life; and that none other could teach men of

the Father, and destroy the worship of idols, save the Word, that orders all things and is alone the true only-begotten Son of the Father.'

The reasons that Athanasius gives for Christ's advent ought to be acceptable to all Christians. Christ came to restore the divine image, to save us from (spiritual) corruption and to give us a true knowledge of the Father. Yet Athanasius fails to show that Christ could not have achieved these ends if he had not been divine. Let us suppose that Christ was merely a man. Even so he could have revealed God's true nature by his teaching. Also he could have lived a life of complete obedience to God by the aid of the Holy Spirit. Through the same Spirit we could imitate him and so achieve spiritual perfection. Alternatively God could have chosen to save the human race by a series of holy men of whom each would exhibit spiritual perfection in a manner suited to the *ethos* of his time and place. There could have been many 'Christs' (and not one of them necessarily in ancient Palestine). Again, God might have saved us by other means that we cannot conceive. To deny this possibility is to claim a presumptuous degree of insight into his wisdom and power.

Other theologians, however, have been content to claim that the Incarnation is the most suitable means of atonement. This view was held by Aquinas. In his *Summa Theologica* 3, 1, 2 he considers the question whether it was necessary for the restoration of the human race that God should become man. He begins by distinguishing between two kinds of necessity:-[16]

'A means is judged necessary either because the end cannot be secured without it, thus food is necessary for life, or because the end is better and more conveniently reached through it, thus a horse is necessary for a journey. The first kind of necessity does not enter into the Incarnation, for God's almighty power could have restored human nature in many other ways. The necessity was of the second kind, for, as Augustine declares, other ways were not closed to God, who equally commands everything, but no means was more suitable for healing our woe.'

Aquinas proceeds to consider the second kind of necessity with reference to our advancement in good and our withdrawal from evil. He states five ways in whch the Incarnation is a specially effective means of producing goodness in us:-

'Under the first heading let us take faith. We have better guarantee when we believe that God himself is speaking to us. Augustine says that it was that we might set forth more trustfully to the truth that the Son of God, having become man, founded and built faith. Next, take hope, so highly lifted up, for, as Augustine asks, what better could have raised our hope than this proof of God's deep love for us, what more cogent than the Son of God deigning to become our partner in human nature? Then take charity, thereby strongly enkindled, for, as Augustine also asks, what mightier cause is there for the Lord's coming than to show us his love? He adds, that if we have been slow to love in the past let us now hasten to love in return. Fourthly, take right conduct, where an example is set us. Augustine points out that men can be seen but should not be followed, God should be followed but cannot be seen, and therefore

God became man that he might both be seen and followed. Finally, with regard to our full sharing in the divinity, which is our true end and bliss bestowed on us through Christ's manhood, Augustine says that he became man that man might become God.'

Aquinas then gives the same number of reasons why the Incarnation is a specially effective means of rescuing us from evil.

'Under the second heading, let us first meditate on how man is taught by the Incarnation not to rank the devil above himself or to be cowed by the author of evil. Augustine reflects that when a human nature can be so joined to God that there is but one person there, let no proud spirits vaunt themselves above men because they are unearthly and without flesh. Secondly, we are taught how great is human dignity lest we sully it with sin. Augustine says that God has now shown us the high place human nature holds in creation, for he entered into it by genuinely becoming man. And Pope Leo cries, Know your worth, O Christian; you are made a partner of the divine nature: refuse, then, to return to your former worthlessness by degenerate intercourse. Thirdly, in order to do away with our presumption, the grace of God, says Augustine, is commended in Jesus Christ, through no preceding merits of our own. Fourthly, man's pride, says Augustine in the same place, his greatest hindrance to clinging to God, is rebuked and cured by humility so great. Fifthly, in order to free us from the bondage of sin: this, says Augustine, should be done in such a way that the devil is overthrown by the justice of a man, and by Christ making satisfaction for us. A mere man could not make satisfaction for the whole human race, and this is no office of God's. How right, then, that our Saviour should be both God and man. Pope Leo says that weakness is assumed by strength, lowliness by majesty, mortality by immortality, in order that one and the same mediator between God and men might die in the one and rise in the other. Unless he were God, he could not have brought the remedy; unless he were man, he could not have set the example.'

Nearly all the reasons Aquinas gives are valid. The only questionable ones are those that imply belief in the Devil and in the 'satisfaction' theory of atonement. It is the last of the positive reasons I want to stress. Aquinas (echoing many of the Fathers) says that Christ became man that we might become God. This language of 'deification' must be suitably interpreted so as to avoid any ontological confusion between the Creator and his creatures. Nevertheless it signifies the truth that Christ confers on his disciples a supernatural mode of existence. Hence even if God could have chosen other means of salvation the means that he has in fact chosen is superior to any other. If we take atonement to mean, ultimately, at-one-ment or union with God we can affirm with certainty that we cannot achieve any union with him that is as close as the union made possible by his Incarnation.

3. There is the question of the salvation available to non-Christians. Here we must come to terms with the following facts. On the one hand, because God desires the salvation of all men and because Christ is the incarnation of the Word by whom all things were made, we cannot set

a priori limits to the extent to which non-Christian theists can be aware of sin and experience God's saving power. On the other hand, to abandon the claim for Christ's indispensability as the mediator of salvation would be to reject the New Testament's whole conception of the Gospel. This antinomy can be resolved as follows. First, Christians can justly claim that Christ, as God incarnate, constitutes the most appropriate mode of divine salvation; that it is an all-sufficient mode and, for them, the only effective one; and that it fulfils all the modes that the non-Christian is able to experience. Again, there is the fact that many non-Christian theists have been converted to Christianity because they have been unable to find in their own forms of theism redemption from sin and the power to achieve full communion with God. Paul is the prime example. Yet the final resolution of the antinomy consists in the fact that the goal of atonement is union with Christ. What would apply to a sinless person would also apply to a non-Christian's experience of God's saving power. Just as the first person would lack supernatural perfection, so the second person, in so far as he lacks the same perfection, would also lack the fulness of the salvation that God offers us in Christ.

The indispensability of Christ for full, complete, salvation emerges with greater particularity from a consideration of knowledge, love, and Christ's eschatological significance.

Knowledge of God is the basis of union with him. If, then, he became man, a person who does not believe in the Incarnation does not know him fully. Here it must be noted that the Word did not discard his humanity; he retains it eternally in a glorified state. Hence lack of belief in the Incarnation is ignorance, not merely of God's presence on earth for a brief period of ancient history, but of the human form in which he exists now and for ever. Furthermore, belief in the Incarnation leads to belief in the Trinity. Through the Incarnation, and through it alone, we learn that God's nature takes the three-fold form of Father, Son and Holy Spirit.

Love, too, is an essential element in man's union with God. Yet love is proportioned to knowledge. We love a person in a manner and with an intensity that are exacted by those of his qualities and acts with which we are acquainted. Thus a son's love for his mother is determined by his knowledge of the sacrifices she has made on his behalf. This truth is pre-eminently applicable to the Incarnation. As the Johannine literature continually affirms, Christians' love for God is constituted in its essential nature by the fact that it is a response to his love in becoming man for their sake.

Lastly, there is the New Testament's affirmation that God intends to fulfil all history in Christ. The crucial passage is Ephesians 1. 7-10. Verses 7 and 8 speak of the atonement that Christ offers to believers within this present life. 'In him we have redemption through his blood, the forgiveness of our trespasses, according to the riches of his grace which he has lavished upon us.' Verses 9 and 10 then place redemption in a cosmic setting. 'For he has made known to us in all wisdom and insight the mystery of his will, according to his purpose which he set forth in Christ as a plan for the fulness of time, to unite all things in him.'

This statement of Christ's eschatological role is necessitated by the doctrine of the Incarnation. If Christ is identical with the Word by whom all things exist he must also be the one in whom they will be fulfilled. He who is Alpha must also be Omega. So far as our relation to the Word is concerned it must be objectively and absolutely true that in our beginning is our end. Therefore even if there are many ways of salvation Christ is the only final way. Any other way must be ultimately included in and transformed by him.

Two questions remain. First, would God have become man if man had not sinned? In the Middle Ages the question was answered affirmatively by Scotus and negatively by Aquinas. It has been said in favour of an affirmative answer that if God is love he must desire the highest good for his creatures; but the highest good for human creatures is that they should achieve the supernatural destiny of union with God incarnate; and so God must have become man. Although the argument is attractive it is not, I think, conclusive. In general, no human person can know (as against opine) that God would have acted in this or that way in other circumstances. In particular, I doubt whether the reason I have given in support of the Scotist view is finally cogent. To say that God would not have conferred supernatural perfection on sinless creatures need not imply any lack of generosity on his part. It lies wholly within his hidden wisdom to decide what forms of perfection he will create and in what modes they will reflect his glory. Moreover, his love is always infinite and unvarying. This means that even if he had not become man in a sinless world he would still have loved men infinitely, and he would still have ceaselessly sought their highest good in terms of their created nature. In any case it is doubtful whether the premise of the question is valid. The premise is 'if man had not sinned'. However, if the advent of sin was virtually inevitable in our world the hypothesis is inadmissible. And to think of a world in which sin could not arise is to think of a world that is totally different from the one we inhabit. The whole question, I suggest, is a profitless one. The only world we know is a sinful one, and the only act of incarnation we know is one that was a remedy for sin. Thus we are brought back to the paradox: *O felix culpa.*

My second question is one that I could have raised at various points in the preceding chapters but which I choose to raise here because it is especially relevant to the doctrine of the Atonement. All views of the Atonement agree that Christ's mental and physical sufferings constituted an essential element in our redemption; and I have followed the Fathers in maintaining that the Atonement gains its whole meaning from the Incarnation. Must we then say that God himself suffered in his own nature? The answer given by the Fathers was a negative one. In Christ, they said, God suffered, not in his divine nature, but solely in the human nature he assumed. Some modern theologians wish to hold that God suffered in his divine nature also. I do not think it is necessary to hold this. We cannot attribute any of Christ's human experiences to his divine nature by strict identification without confusing the natures and falling into absurdity. The absurdity in this case is that we should then have to say that the incorporeal and incorruptible God felt the pain of crucifixion and then died. The most we can rationally say is that there was a *counterpart* to Christ's human suffering in his divinity. But we can say this only by a generally theistic inference to the effect that if God is love he must be pained by our sins and share our sufferings. Is, then, this inference correct? I see no way of establishing that it is so; for none of us has access to God's inner life; and so none of us is able to determine the limits of analogical predication in terms of God's immediate experience. Also even those who feel confident in affirming that God suffers must admit that his sufferings differ vastly from ours in two respects. First, if God suffers his sufferings have no ground in his own nature that is constituted by the joy that he experiences within his own interchange of love as Father, Son and Holy Spirit. If he suffers his sufferings must be wholly imaginative, wholly vicarious. Secondly, his sufferings must be immediately and wholly transfigured by his joy - a joy in which Christians hope to participate for their eternal bliss. I therefore suggest that speculation here too is pointless. All we know and all we need to know is that God so loved us that he bore the whole weight of our sin and suffering in the human nature he assumed for our salvation.[17]

In conclusion I shall state three principles of soteriology. They all involve matters of theological proportion.

1. It is important to maintain a balance between the objective and the subjective aspects of atonement. Throughout the theistic form of religion objectivity and subjectivity are correlative. On the one hand God is an objective reality; he exists independently of the human mind. On the other hand he cannot be known except by the subjective response of faith. The complementary nature of object and subject also characterizes Christian revelation. God's revelation of himself in Christ is an objective presence that confronts us and over which we have no control. Yet this revelation can be apprehended only by an act of faith that is itself revelatory in so far as it is due to the illumination of the Holy Spirit. Similarly in the eucharist although Christ is objectively present, his power cannot be received without repentance and faith. So too the Atonement is both objective and subjective.

First, the Atonement is objective. It is grounded in the life, death and exaltation of Christ as the incarnate Son. In Christ God accomplished all that is required from his side for our salvation. Therefore we can call the atonement that Christ effected a 'finished work'. Yet this work is not effective for us unless it is appropriated by faith. John Macquarrie cogently states the subjective aspect of the Atonement thus. 'Man cannot be saved as, let us say, a burning building can be saved, by an action that is entirely external to him. This would be to make the whole matter sub-personal. Man is saved only in so far as he responds to and appropriates into his existence the saving activity that is directed towards him. So we must criticize any attempt to represent the atonement as a "transaction" that goes on outside those who are at stake in the matter.'[18]

2. In interpreting Christ's saving work we must do equal justice to his deity and to his humanity. He saves us both as God and as man. He saves us as God because the Incarnation was an unsurpassable revelation of divine love, and because his whole human life was constituted by the hypostatic union. Christ saves us also as man. It was by his perfect obedience that he proved himself to be God's incarnate Son, and became the first member of a new creation. His obedience was not automatic or easy. It was achieved through constant acts of self-surrender; and its final cost was the agony of the Cross.

3. We must interpret Christ's saving work in the light of his life, his death, his resurrection and Pentecost equally. A defect in many presentations of the Atonement is that they restrict it to Christ's death. But the death was a consequence of the life, and the Resurrection was a consequence of the death. Christ's death was the inevitable outcome of the obedience that characterized his life. The Resurrection signified his victory over the very forces of evil that had crucified him. Lastly, through the Holy Spirit he communicates to believers the crucified and risen life that, in his exalted state, he presents eternally to the Father on their behalf.

[1] Acts 4. 12.
[2] Jn. 14. 6.
[3] Jn. 3. 16.
[4] Rom. 5. 8.
[5] *De. Trin.* 8. 7.
[6] Gal. 2. 20.
[7] *The Absolute and the Atonement* (London 1971, p 1888).
[8] *Forgiveness and Reconciliation* (London 1948, p 195). The ideas of satisfaction, propitiation and penal substitution have either no or scarcely any foundation in the N.T. The first and second have none at all. The N.T. writers never affirm or even imply that Christ's death satisfied God's justice or propitiated his wrath. Thus in Romans 5. 9 Paul says that Christ saves us from God's wrath, not that he placated it. The third idea can be supported from the N.T. only by pressing a few texts beyond their necessary meaning. Thus when Paul says in Gal. 3. 13 that Christ became a curse for us, all that the context requires us to affirm (in terms of Deut. 21. 23 to which Paul refers) is that Christ died the death of a criminal. The same can be said of Paul's enigmatic statement in 2 Cor. 5. 21 that God made Christ 'to be sin who knew no sin'. Appeal is also sometimes made to Christ's cry from the Cross: 'My God, my God, why hast thou forsaken me?' But this cry can be taken to signify simply Christ's sense of desolation due to his rejection by God's chosen people and to his horror at the spiritual blindness that caused this rejection. The message of these texts - as indeed of many other texts - is that Christ, as the eternal Son, identified himself wholly with our humanity in order to save us from our sins. Yet in this self-identification he did not pay a penalty that our sins had incurred; he offered (according to the total testimony of the N.T.) a free deliverance from our sins by his victory over the sin that crucified him.

[9] *Byzantine Theology* (New York 1974, p 171).

[10] London 1962.

[11] p 455.

[12] p 459.

[13] p 460.

[14] Ps. 51 4.

[15] *De Inc.* 20 (English trans., Westminister Press, 1954, pp 73-4).

[16] The translations are taken from Gilby's *Theological Texts* (Oxford 1955, pp 277-9).

[17] Of all the attributes traditionally ascribed to God impassibility (in the sense of an incapacity to experience pain) is the one that has been most criticized in this century. Although I once held that God experienced pain I am no longer sure, for the reason I have given, that this view is correct. I have become increasingly impressed by Von Hügel's defence of belief in divine impassibility in terms of his own experience. This defence surely makes it impossible for a Christian to dismiss the belief as merely an 'hellenization' of primitive Christianity. However, the area of disagreement here is very narrow and need not disturb our common faith. All Christians can agree on these propositions: that God, out of his infinate love for us, suffered in our nature on our behalf; that if he suffers in his divine nature his sufferings, being wholly imaginative and vicarious in relation to a created order that is wholly distinct from him, cannot change him (as suffering so often changes us) for better or for worse; and that, if he thus suffers, what finally matters for us is the transfiguration of his sufferings by his eternal joy.

[18] *Principles of Christian Theology* (London 1977, p 316).

CHAPTER 7
GRACE AND FREE WILL

This chapter is both a sequel to and a supplementation of the preceding one. 'Salvation' and 'grace' have always been closely associated in Christian theology. The association was succinctly stated by the author of the epistle to the Ephesians when he wrote: 'By grace you have been saved'.[1] Equally 'grace' has been associated with 'free will'. However, within the theology of the Western Church grace and free will have sometimes been regarded as co-existing within a tension and even as being in conflict with each other. I hope to show that there is no such tension, still less conflict. Yet first I must define 'grace'.

'Grace' is a complex concept. Manuals of theology sometimes make minute distinctions between different kinds of grace. In my view these distinctions are often neither theologically nor spiritually helpful. It is sufficient to distinguish between three main meanings that 'grace', when applied to God, can have in a Christian context. (a) It can mean the unmerited kindness and generosity revealed in the salvation that God freely offers us in Christ. This is its dominant meaning in the New Testament, especially the Pauline epistles. (b) 'Grace' can mean God's action in strengthening and sanctifying the sinner. This meaning accords with common usage. When the Christian says: 'Grant me thy grace, O Lord' he means 'Strengthen me and make me good'. (c) 'Grace' can mean 'created grace' (*gratia creata*) or 'infused grace' (*gratia infusa*) - that is, a created power that God infuses into the soul as the principle of a supernatural life and the ground of the Christian virtues. I shall begin by examining the third sense of grace both because it is the most difficult to grasp and because it is, in my view, untenable. In order to criticize it fairly I shall quote from an account of it given by R. W. Gleason in a book entitled simply *Grace*.[2]

Gleason begins by noting that this sense of grace is not found in the Bible. In the Old Testament the nearest parallel to the Pauline sense of *charis* is the Hebrew *hesed* which, when applied to God, signifies 'his persistent, devoted, loving-kindness to those to whom he has covenanted himself'.[3] This meaning of *hesed* is fulfilled in the New Testament's description of the divine *charis* revealed in Christ. Thus in the Pauline epistles 'we see the essential meaning of grace as the gratuitous favour of God manifest in the economy of redemption'.[4] The concept of *gratia creata* arose with the Latin Fathers, especially Augustine, for whom grace came to mean 'a spirit, a force, an élan by which God directs and draws man to eternal life'.[5] Gleason adheres to this concept in its scholastic formulations. Grace, he maintains, is 'a permanent created gift inhering in the soul'.[6] Again 'it continues to exist in the soul, not as a series of transient aids given to man but as something like a new soul - a permanent, durable principle of activity'.[7] It is 'a unique accident', 'an ontological reality', 'a positive entity'.[8]

I find this concept untenable for the following reasons. First, it is unintelligible. Created grace is, presumably, personal; but it is not identical with either the divine nature or a human nature. What, then, can it be? Secondly, such grace would be incompatible with the integrity of the human person. If it existed alongside the normal faculties of a person it would produce a split personality. Yet if it merged with them it would lose its special character as well as interfere with their true functioning. Thirdly, it does not bear any necessary relation to Christ's person and saving work. Some accounts of it contain no reference to Christ at all. Lastly, the concept of created grace could easily be taken to imply that there is a gulf between God and man that needs to be bridged by an intermediary. The need for such intermediaries was acutely felt by both Jews and Greeks at the time when Christianity arose. Yet if we understand creation and redemption rightly we shall see that the need does not exist. Within the order of creation God is wholly present to every man by his creative energy. Within the order of redemption he is wholly present through the Holy Spirit who re-creates believers by communicating to them the life of the exalted Christ. Hence when the writers of the New Testament want to indicate God's redemptive power within the Christian they do so simply with reference either to Christ or to the Holy Spirit. These references are sufficient. The idea of a created intermediary is superfluous.

The Holy Spirit does not add anything to the structure of the soul that he indwells. In speaking of salvation as supernatural we must here make three distinctions. We must distinguish between the cause, the medium and the effect of God's presence in Christians. The cause (the Holy Spirit) is supernatural. So also is the effect (the transformation of the soul in the image of Christ). But the medium is wholly natural. It consists simply in our created faculties. The Holy Spirit changes creatures (as Mersch puts it) by causing them to exist as they were but in a more perfect way.

We are left, then, with the first and second senses of grace. So far as the first sense is concerned my own view is this. On the one hand this sense is not indispensable. In place of 'grace' we can use, simply, 'love' to indicate God's kindness in sending Christ to be our Saviour. 'Love' was the word that the fourth evangelist used, and it was God's 'covenant-love' for Israel that Christ fulfilled. On the other hand we ought to retain 'grace' in this sense partly because of its importance in Pauline theology, but mainly because it indicates as no other word can do, the unmerited character of our salvation. Yet is is necessary to add one qualification and one addition. The qualification is that grace is not one of God's attributes. It is simply his love expressed in his salvation of sinners. The addition is that Christ, as the incarnate Son, was not merely the instrument of God's grace; he actually embodied it. Hence Paul refers interchangeably to the grace of God and the grace of Christ.

There remains the second sense of grace, according to which it signifies God's strengthening and sanctifying power. This sense is so deeply entrenched in Christian language that it is probably ineradicable. In any case it has the advantage of indicating that God's presence in the soul is a supernatural gift that is always unmerited. Yet it must be used with care. This gift does not take the form of some strange substance entitled *gratia creata*. It is the gift of the Father's own nature incarnated in the Son and mediated through the Holy Spirit. Hence in every circumstance the prayer 'Grant me thy grace' must be capable of being translated as 'Give me, Father, of your unmerited generosity and through your Holy Spirit a participation in the life of your beloved Son'.

I maintain, therefore, that the concept of grace should be retained but that it should be used only in the first and second senses I have given - and then only with the qualifications I have stated. It follows, moreover, from what I have said that grace, in both these senses, is identical with God's presence in Christ. The kindness of God revealed in Christ is identical with the divine nature that Christ incarnated. The strengthening and sanctifying power that Christians experience is identical with the power of the risen Christ mediated to believers by the Holy Spirit. On this crucial point I have the support of T. F. Torrance whose words will help to establish a link with my interpretation of the Atonement. 'Grace', Torrance writes, 'is not something that can be proliferated in many forms; nor is it something that we can have more or less of, as if grace could be construed in quantitative terms. Grace is whole and indivisible because it is identical with the personal self-giving of God to us in his Son. It is identical with Jesus Chirst. Thus it would be just as wrong to speak of many graces as of many Christs, or of sacramental grace as of a sacramental Christ, or of created grace as of a created Christ'.[9] A little later in the same essay Torrance expands this judgment thus. 'Grace is the self-giving of Christ to us in which he both redeems and recreates us, such a self-giving that he unites us to himself and makes us share in his human nature, and in him share in the very life and love of God himself'.[10]

Any account of grace (and thereby of salvation) would be incomplete without a reference to the closely connected concept of justification. This concept too has been interpreted in three main ways. Of these the first was originally stated by Paul and is best approached through the verb 'to justify'. The latter, for him, had a variety of meanings of which the chief are 'to make, or put, right', 'to acquit' and 'to deliver'. Hence his assertion that we are justified by God's grace can be paraphrased as follows. Through his unmerited generosity revealed in Chirst God delivers us from sin by an act of free acquittal (or forgiveness) and so restores us to a right relation with himself. Secondly, in medieval theology justification meant (as it never meant for Paul) 'to make righteous or holy', and it was associated with the concept of *gratia infusa*. God justifies by infusing grace into the soul and so transforming it. This meaning was given to justification by Aquinas and was endorsed by the Council of Trent. The third meaning originated with the Reformers and is indicated by the word 'imputation'. God imputes the righteousness, the holiness, of Christ to believing sinners although they do not actually possess it. God thus regards their sin as being 'covered' by Christ's righteousness so that he is able to accept them as his adopted sons.

The concept of imputation is, I hold, untenable. It is a legal fiction that is incompatible with the personal and moral nature of the relation between God and man. It is also objectionable on two further grounds. By placing a condition on God's acceptance of the sinner it paradoxically undermines the belief in God's free forgiveness that the Reformers were so anxious to defend. Also, in a way that is contrary to their intention, it can encourage the view that if Christ's righteousness is imputed to us we need not be too concerned with its impartation as the ground of godly living. Certainly we can appropriately ask God to regard us, not as the sinners we now are, but as the saints we can become through our union with Christ. This is the meaning I should attach to these words taken from an often sung hymn: 'Look, Father, look on his anointed face, and only look on us as found in him'. Yet God's acceptance of us as sinners is wholly free and does not in the least depend on the imputation to us of a holiness that is not our own.

The Pauline sense of justification ought to be acceptable to all Christians; for it states an essential element in the New Testament's understanding of redemption. Furthermore this sense and the later medieval sense are, though different in the ways I have indicated, to a large extent complementary. On the one hand Paul certainly thought that justification would lead to sanctification through participation in the life of the risen Christ. On the other hand Aquinas and the Tridentine fathers held that justification is accompanied by the forgiveness of sins. Nevertheless I think that 'justification' should be restricted to its Pauline sense for several reasons. This sense emphasizes the unmerited nature of divine forgiveness. Even as sinners we are reconciled to God by his grace. Also if we take 'to justify' to mean 'to make righteous' and so equate justification with sanctification we rob 'justification' of its distinctive meaning. Lastly, the equation is historically associated with the concept of *gratia creata*. This concept (so I have argued) is not needed in order to explain the process of sanctification that justification initiates.

I turn now to the question of free will. By free will I mean quite simply the capacity to choose between X and Y without any antecedent necessity to choose either of them; so that if a person chose X instead of Y he could have chosen Y in the same circumstances. Free will can be experienced in many spheres, but only two are relevant to my purpose: morality and religion. In the first sphere free will signifies a capacity to choose between good and evil or between duty and inclination. In the second sphere it signifies a capacity to accept or to reject God's claim upon us. From a Christian standpoint it especially signifies a capacity to accept or to reject God's saving will revealed in Christ. These two spheres are closely interrelated. On the one hand the moral law is itself an expression of God's will even if it is not recogized as such. On the other hand the life of faith involves moral choices continually.

I shall begin by stating what I consider to be two theological principles. First, Christianity presupposes free will in both the religious and the moral spheres. If our wills were not free in the religious sphere there would be no point in preaching the Gospel. Such preaching would do no more than intensify a pre-existing tendency to accept or to reject God's Word. There would be no genuine offer of salvation, no genuine invitation to eternal life. And this would affect the preaching of Jesus and his apostles quite as much as that of their successors. Equally Christianity presupposes free will in the moral sphere. If our wills were not morally free we should not be responsible for our actions and so accountable to God. I shall amplify these assertions later.

Secondly, grace and free will are not necessarily incompatible. On the contrary they are wholly compatible according to the first and second interpretations of grace I give. We are free to accept or to reject God's forgiving love. Equally we are free to accept or to reject the Spirit's sanctifying power. The Spirit is not an impersonal force that overwhelms our wills. He is a personal agent who respects our freedom throughout his redemptive activity. Salvation is due both to God's unmerited initiative and to man's free response. Hence Paul tells the Philippians: 'work out your own salvation with fear and trembling; for God is at work in you, both to will and to work for his good pleasure'.[11]

Yet the existence of free will has been denied both by philosophers and by theologians. Philosophical forms of determinism (with the exception of the Marxist form) have not much influenced ordinary people. Theological determinism has had much wider effects. It has coloured many Christians' whole view of God's will and man's destiny. Also it has been held by many theologians who are rightfully included in the first rank of the Church's teachers. Nevertheless, a theologian who seeks to refute determinism must begin with its secular forms; for if these are true any free response to God on either the moral or the religious plane becomes impossible.

Although secular determinism has had some philosophically acute defenders I am convinced that it is invalid on the following grounds.

1. There are various forms of determinism: social, economic and psychological. Determinists often fail to make it clear which form they are advocating. If determinism deserves to be considered, all forms of it deserve consideration. Yet all forms cannot be simultaneously and totally valid. We cannot be at the same time totally determined by (say) both economic and psychological factors although we could be partly determined by one set of factors and partly by another. All I am claiming is that determinists frequently fail to clarify this point.

2. Can we ever have sufficient evidence for holding that determinism is true? There are at least two reasons for supposing that we could never

have it. First, it is impossible to submit human beings to the same extensive scrutiny to which natural scientists submit physical phenomena in their search for causal laws. Apart from any moral inhibitions that may prevent some forms of experiment, human beings are too complicated and various for us ever to be sure that we have taken all factors into account. In fact determinists base their claims on antecedent theory quite as much as on empirical investigation. Secondly, there is always counter-evidence in the form of the ineradicable conviction held by so many people that their wills are free in at any rate some areas of moral choice. Although this is a subjective datum in contrast with the objective data to which the determinist appeals it is as real to the experient as those causal laws that govern the physical realm.

3. If determinism were true how could the illusion of free will arise? If we are wholly determined why are we not conscious of being so? These questions gain additional force from the fact that we feel ourselves able to resist those very forces by which according to determinism our actions are invariably caused. The sense of free will cannot be plausibly attributed to 'wish-fulfilment'. Admittedly it may seem desirable in so far as it raises us above physical nature. Yet is also imposes on us an existential burden together with a burden of guilt on those occasions when we have misused our freedom of choice.

4. Determinism is incompatible with a great deal of our moral language. In particular it is incompatible with the concepts of obligation and moral responsibility. I cannot be obliged to do X unless I am free to do it simply because it is my duty and not because I am determined by other factors. Of course obligation is itself a determining factor in so far as it is a form of constraint. However the constraint is a unique one; and a sign of its uniqueness is that it leaves a person free either to accept or to reject it. Equally I cannot be morally responsible for an action that I was compelled to perform even if the compulsion proceeds from my own nature and so is an act of self-determination. And if I am not responsible for an action I cannot be blamed for it.

5. Chiefly, however, determinism is self-stultifying. If my mental processes are totally determined, I am totally determined either to accept or to reject determinism. But if the sole reason for my believing or not believing X is that I am causally determined to believe it I have no ground for holding that my judgment is true or false. J. R. Lucas has put the point cogently with reference to Marxist and Freudian forms of determinism thus. 'The Marxist who says that all ideologies have no independent validity and merely reflect the class interests of those who hold them can be told that in that case his Marxist views merely express the economic interests of his class, and have no more claim to be judged true or valid than any other view. So too the Freudian, if he makes out that everybody else's philosophy is merely the consequence of childhood experiences, is, by parity of reasoning, revealing merely

his delayed response to what happened to him when he was a child.'[12] Lucas then makes the same point with regard to a person who maintains, more generally, that our behaviour is totally determined by heredity and environment. 'If what he says is true, he says it merely as the result of his heredity and environment, and of nothing else. He does not hold his determinist views because they are true, but because he has such-and-such a genetic make-up, and has received such-and-such stimuli; that is, not because the *structure* of the universe is such-and-such but only because the configuration of only one part of the universe, together with the structure of the determinist's brain, is such as to produce that result.'[13]

The exact force of this criticism is sometimes missed. Certainly on deterministic premises determinism may be true. But we should not have any grounds for affirming that it is true or therefore for knowing that it is so. In order to obtain these grounds we must be free from all determining factors in order to assess the evidence according to its own worth. This principle applies to the assessment of all truth-claims (including those of Christianity). Freedom from determining factors is therefore required in the cognitive as much as in the moral sphere.

A frequently urged objection to the concept of moral freedom is that unless an act is causally determined it is purely random and so unintelligible. The objection is invalid. It presupposes that the only form of causation is the form that is objectively verifiable and subsumable under universal laws. However, moral freedom is an act of self-causation that can be recognized only by subjective awareness, and that by its nature cannot be included within any law enabling it to be predictable. It is useless to ask for a further description of it; for it is *sui generis*. It is understood by being experienced; but it cannot be explained in terms of anything outside the experience.

I do not claim to have proved with certainty that determinism is false or that libertarianism is true. The position, as I see it, is this. On the one hand the objections to determinism are so strong that we are rationally compelled to withhold assent to it. On the other hand, in view of these objections, a person who finds that the consciousness of freedom is an irreducible datum of his own experience has every right to regard this datum as a reality. In fact I find it impossible to imagine anyone who does not have this experience. Can anyone seriously maintain that he is not aware of having any control over any of his actions in any moment of moral choice? I do not think so.

Yet two qualifications are required. First the area in which moral freedom operates is obviously limited. Our actions are often conditioned by internal and external constraints over which we have no control. And God, being both all-knowing and all-just, does not impute guilt to a person when the latter performs acts that, though objectively sinful, are subjectively unavoidable. Secondly although the ability not to sin (*posse non peccare*) is a form of freedom, the highest form consists in the inability to sin (*non posse peccare*). Yet the latter form will not be achieved until the life to come.

Let us next consider theological determinism. According to this God predestines some to salvation and leaves the rest to damnation. It may well seem self-evident that predestination is incompatible with free-will in the religious sense of man's capacity to accept or to reject God's offer of grace. Nevertheless, Augustine held that the two were compatible. His position is aptly summed up by J. N. D. Kelly as follows. 'Augustine acknowledges that God's omnipotent will, operating on our wills by grace, is irrestistible. But he points out that he works through our wills, the effect being that they freely and spontaneously will what is good. To be more explicit, God knows in advance under the influence of what motives this or that particular will will freely consent to what he proposes for it, and arranges things accordingly. Thus grace accommodates itself to each individual's situation and character and Augustine can claim that, for all the power of grace, it rests with the recipient's will to accept or reject it.'[14]

This attempt to reconcile predestination with free will is surely unacceptable. If God's grace is irresistible we cannot be free to resist it. Admittedly Augustine conceives this irresistibility in terms of an overwhelming attraction, not an impersonal force. Nevertheless, if God so influences my motives and so arranges my circumstances that I am compelled to be attracted by him my freedom of choice is destroyed. Augustine's position here is vitiated (as Kelly's use of the adverb 'spontaneously' shows) by a confusion between two senses of freedom: freedom to choose God or reject him, and freedom from all sinful inclinations so that one inevitably accepts him. It is the first sense that is in question here. If this sense is to be secured we must affirm that however attractive God is we cannot freely choose him unless we deliberately do so in preference to other attractions rooted in our 'fallen' nature.

I shall, then, take it for granted that (as Luther maintained) predestination is incompatible with the existence of free will in the religious sphere. Is, then, belief in predestination acceptable? It is, I submit, totally unacceptable on two grounds. Although I have already stated the first in general terms it merits repetition in this context. If God predestines some to salvation by an irresistible decree the preaching of the Gospel becomes pointless. By 'preaching' I mean any attempt at persuading people to accept or even to consider God's revelation in Christ. The only status preaching could have would be that of a means through which God enacts his predestinating will. Also the idea of predestination portrays God as an arbitrary sovereign. Why does he predestine some instead of others? All believers in predestination are obliged to admit that the reasons for God's choice are utterly inscrutable. This is an intolerable admission. It renders the basis of faith irrational. Of course we can never have a complete understanding of God's acts; but on this view we cannot have any understanding at all of the very act that is the sole ground of our salvation. This objection becomes morally more acute when we remember that God's choice of some is accompanied by his rejection of others. Augustine's reply that God's justice and mercy are vindicated by the fact that all merit condemnation is inadquate. It still leaves us with the question why God elects some and not others for salvation. It is useless to reply further that God's hidden decree is characterized by a 'higher' justice that we cannot fathom; for to invoke a form of justice that has no analogy in human experience is meaningless. Finally, predestinarianism rules out the possibility that all men will ultimately be saved; but this possibility (so I shall later argue) must be allowed.

Fortunately the doctrine of predestination is not the live question that it was in previous ages. Yet if only because it has been held by some among the Church's leading theologians and has been incorporated into confessional formulae it requires consideration. Furthermore my objections to the doctrine apply *mutatis mutandis* to secular determinism. If we are totally determined by (say) our social class or genetic constitution to believe or not to believe in God the commendation of Christianity would merely take the form of eliciting inevitable responses. Even my second objection to predestinarianism has an analogous application to secular determinism. If it is intolerable to believe that God predestines some to salvation by his hidden decree it is also intolerable to suppose that he leaves the salvation of men to the operation of forces over which they have no control.

Moreover, if the human will is free to accept or to reject God's offer of salvation it must also be free on the purely moral plane once the offer of salvation has been accepted. It is inconsistent to affirm on the one hand that we are free to accept God's grace and on the other hand that we are not free to choose between good and evil within the moral life that grace sustains. Conversely, if God predestines us to accept salvation, he must also predestine us to cultivate all those moral dispositions and perform all those moral acts that salvation entails. The moral exhortations of the New Testament are then stultified. Just as predestination in the religious sphere would invalidate apostolic *kerygma* so predestination in the moral sphere would invalidate apostolic *didache.*

I do not wish to deny that in some moments of spiritual illumination God attracts us so strongly that we respond spontaneously to him. Yet two qualifications are required. First, such moments are not caused by a predestinating decree. They express in their own mode a salvation that God offers to all men. Secondly, most Christians find that much more frequently God is not overwhelmingly attractive, but that they must choose deliberately between his will and their own. Although the highest form of freedom is the inabiliy to sin it is achieved only by degrees through the exercise of our ability not to sin through the right use of free will.

A further question arises from my defence of free will. Is it right to affirm that the Christian cooperates with divine grace and contributes to his salvation? I maintain that it is so. Such cooperation is present whenever a person accepts God's grace and seeks to discern or obey his will. We may also rightly affirm that the Christian contributes to his salvation in so far as without his free response he could not be saved. To make these affirmations is entirely compatible with the conviction that God's salvific activity is unmerited. Yet do not the affirmations conflict with the view that we are saved by grace alone (*sola gratia*)? Clearly they do so. And I do not hesitate to say that the view is false. In theological slogans 'alone' is nearly always misleading. Let us consider the two obvious parallels: 'by scripture alone' (*sola scriptura*) and 'by faith alone' (*sola fide*) The Bible cannot stand alone. It needs interpretation by the appropriate methods of historical criticism, by an appeal to Christian tradition and, above all, by the illumination of the Holy Spirit. Again, we are not saved by faith alone, for Christian faith is essentially a response to Christian revelation. So it is with *sola gratia*. Grace presupposes free will. One writer has expressed the logic of the matter by stating that although grace is both a *necessary condition* and the *primary factor* in man's salvation it is not the *sufficient condition* and *only factor*.[15] The same writer proceeds to remind us that the qualification of *sola gratia* does not in the least undermine belief in God's sovereignty; for a man's free choice 'is the exercise of a capacity God has bestowed upon him in creating him and it is possible only as long as God preserves that capacity in being'.[16]

In conclusion there is one point that needs stressing. Let us suppose that we reject the idea of predestination. Nevertheless if we take 'grace' to signify God's sanctifying power made effective through the inner operation of the Holy Spirit, we must be resolute in maintaining that grace leaves moral freedom intact. God does not influence us in our moral choices. These are ours and ours alone. We can validly assert, as Paul asserts, that our salvation is due both to our own efforts and to God's power within us. But we cannot validly affirm that our free choices are simultaneously due to the activity of God. Here I endorse the view held by W. G. Maclagan in his *The Theological Frontier of Ethics*.[17]

Maclagan states the essence of his position thus. 'As regards the self-regulation of the will when faced with a moral challenge, the sheer "making up one's mind" and "setting oneself" to do what seems required of us, not only is there no observable presence - I cannot conceive how there could be - of any power not our own operating within our will, but to suppose that in some unobserved way such a power is in fact operative is to suppose something that is in contradiction with the very idea of free willing.'[18] In relation to the act of moral choice grace, Maclagan contends, is 'environmental', not 'constitutive'. By this he means that although we may obtain help from God in our acts of choice God does not to any degree determine the choice itself. 'All the help we can get remains as it were extraneous to the will: relative to the will it is all *environmental,* not *constitutive,* no matter how intimately environmental it may be.'[19] Maclagan certainly does not wish to set any limits to the operation of divine grace outside the sphere of free choice. He even admits the need for sanctification when he writes that 'we are in some sort polluted'[20] and that 'the will cannot cleanse the man'.[21] He also admits that changes in the soul effected by grace make moral choices easier. But, he rightly insists, these choices are ours alone.

There is one further point on which I agree with Maclagan. He quotes D. M. Baillie for the assertion that when a Christian chooses good he does not 'glow with self-esteem' but attributes his choice to God. However, Maclagan rightly observes that even from a purely moral point of view such self-esteem would be inappropriate for two reasons. First, 'to overcome even the most difficult temptation is still not to do better than I ought'.[22] Secondly, we cannot rest complacently in our choices of good because new choices must still be made in the face of new temptations. Hence vigilance with regard to the future rather than complacency with regard to the past is the proper moral attitude. For both these reasons 'an egocentric attitude is certainly to be deplored'.[23] Maclagan adds that egocentricity and pride can occur in the religious no less than the moral sphere. Here he aptly quotes K. E. Kirk for the view that 'there are those who - though they make little if any use of the time-honoured forms of worship - yet serve their fellows with a humility which puts the ordinary Christian to shame'.[24] Pride and humility are represented among (nominal) Christians and agnostics alike. Their presence or absence has nothing intrinsically to do with the nature of free will.

The Christian has special reasons for not making his choices of good into a ground for complacency or pride. First, even in such choices he depends on God in so far as God's grace makes them easier by strengthening good desires. Secondly, he depends on God for the forgiveness of the wrong choices he has made. And he ought always to be more aware of his moral defeats than of his moral victories. Thirdly, he depends on God for the eradication of his sinful impulses and his achievement of moral perfection partly in this life and fully in the life to come.

Yet may we not rightly ask for God's grace (in the sense of his help and sanctifying power) in moments of moral choice? Certainly we may do so. Such requests proceed from the heart of Christianity. However, what we should mean by them is, not that God should determine the choice itself, but that he should strengthen our good desires so that we either spontaneously perform the good or find the choice of the good easier. In so far as evil inclinations remain our final choice between good and evil is ours alone. Moreover, in any moral situation the Christian is free either to ask or not to ask for God's help. His moral freedom in this respect exemplifies his general freedom to accept or to reject the grace that God continually offers.[25]

[1] Eph. 2. 5.
[2] London 1962.
[3] p 20.
[4] p 51

[5] p 60
[6] p 67.
[7] p 71.
[8] p 233.
[9] *Theology in Reconstruction* (London 1965, pp 182-3).
[10] p 185.
[11] Philip. 2. 12-13.
[12] *The Freedom of the Will* (Oxford 1970, p 114).
[13] *Ibid.*
[14] *Early Christian Doctrines*, p 368.
[15] G. F. Thomas, in his *Christian Ethics and Moral Philosophy* (New York 1955, p 209).
[16] *Ibid.*
[17] London 1961
[18] p 111.
[19] p 115.
[20] p 129.
[21] p 130.
[22] p 139.
[23] p 140.
[24] *Ibid.*
[25] It is no less necessary to preserve the reality of human freedom in the cognitive sphere. When we say that the Holy Spirit 'moves' the soul to faith in Christ by a supernatural activity (so that Christian faith is itself a supernatural act) we must remember that in his work of illumination the Spirit always awaits our free response. In particular we are always free either to give our attention to or to withold it from the manifold 'signs' of God's presence in Christ. Admittedly once we recognize this presence the recognition seems inevitable. Yet this is only because the recognition of all truth seems inevitable when it has been obtained. It is not due to a cognitively predestinating act of God. Moreover, just as our moral response to Christ must be continually repeated if our sanctification is to be assured, so our recognitional response must be repeated, in the face of possible doubt, if the cognitive basis of faith is to be maintained.

CHAPTER 8
THE SOUL AND IMMORTALITY

Throughout the centuries Christians have believed that each human person consists in a soul and body; that the soul survives the death of the body; and that its future life will be immortal. My first question is whether there is in each person a mind or soul that is ontologically distinct from the body. I shall then ask two further questions. Is belief in the existence of the soul necessary for belief in the continued existence of a person after death, and is the existence of a disembodied soul conceivable? But before proceeding I must clarify a point of terminology. I shall treat 'mind' and 'soul' as equivalents. I shall use both to signify the totality of a person in his non-material aspects. I do not see any advantage in distinguishing between the two and restricting them to separate spheres. At the same time I recognize that 'soul' is often the more natural word to use in a religious context (that is, when we consider mind as an entity that bears God's image and so is capable of enjoying eternal communion with him).

First, then, is the soul or mind distinct from the body? Undeniably there is a correlation between the mind and the body, and even a partial dependence of the former on the latter. The brain is the condition of all mental activity; and some mental states are directly caused by physical ones. Furthermore we communicate with each other through our bodily acts, especially speech. Yet for the following reasons I am convinced that mind is not reducible to matter in the form of either external behaviour or internal brain-processes.

(a) There is a linguistic and conceptual impropriety in applying physical properties to mental states (for example, in affirming 'this thought is triangular'). Admittedly we sometimes apply mental properties to physical acts. Thus we say 'that was a clever remark'. Yet we do not mean that the noise was clever. We mean that the intention behind it and so that its meaning were clever. Similarly when we say that a move in chess is astute, we mean, not that the movement of the player's hand was astute, but that his reasoning was so.

(b) If mental acts were reducible to bodily ones we could not distinguish between intelligent and non-intelligent behaviour. Exactly the same behaviour is compatible with both the presence and the absence of intention. Thus at any moment in a game of chess I (who cannot play the game at all) may, by accident, make the same move as the one that would have been made by a skilled player. To take a more striking example, if mind were not other than its physical expressions we could not distinguish between a parrot's utterance of a name and a human utterance of it. Yet we do thus distinguish and, because of the distinction, regard the parrot's utterance as 'uncanny'.

(c) The identity of mind and brain is unverifiable. John Hick puts the point thus with reference to Norman Malcolm's statement of it. 'But how could we possibly locate a mental event in space, other than by simply begging the question at issue and assuming that in locating the brain event we have thereby located the mental event? We can have evidence that we are pointing to the brain correlate of a certain thought; but we need further evidence for the identity of the thought with its brain correlate. And not only is there no such evidence, but it seems impossible to conceive what such evidence might consist of.'[1]

(d) This logical point is confirmed by a factual one. The processes of the brain are homogeneous; they are all of the same 'stuff'. Therefore they cannot account for the qualitative difference between mental acts and between mental dispositions. Thus even if we can correlate a thought with an element in the brain this element cannot be equated with the thought because the same element (or the same type of element) can be correlated with thoughts that are vastly dissimilar.

(e) There is the fact of subjective experience. Let us take, as a rudimentary example, pain and, as a universally familiar example of it, toothache. The feeling of pain can never be physically identified. Thus however exhaustively a dentist examines the pathological condition of my teeth he never comes across anything he can call a pain. The most he can affirm is that a dental state is the cause of my pain. Hence there is a linguistic absurdity in saying: 'the dentist found a cyst and a pain'. My pain is purely private in the sense that it is inaccessible to anyone else's observation. Certainly there may be physical manifestations of it. Thus if the dentist touches a nerve I may wince; but my wincing is a sign of my pain, not the pain itself. There is a twofold proof that the wincing and the pain are not identical. First, I could wince in exactly the same way if I were not in pain (as an actor might wince in playing the part of someone in pain). Secondly, the difference between the manifestations of pain and the pain itself is implied by our normal thought-processes and linguistic usage. Thus a dentist would infer that if I winced I must be in pain. The inferential form of the dentist's judgment indicates that the wincing and the pain are not identical.

(f) Our moral judgments imply a difference between mental states and physical behaviour. If there were no such difference we could not distinguish between real and apparent goodness. Paul stated this distinction as follows: 'If I give away all I have, and if I deliver my body to be burned, but have not charity I gain nothing'.[2] A truly charitable act can proceed only from a charitable disposition that is other than the act and that imparts to it its moral quality. This distinction is not merely a notional one. We have all known acts that, though outwardly the same, have been performed with diverse motives and intentions.

(g) If mind is identical with the body determinism is inevitable, as H. D. Lewis observes thus. 'If our bodily states and our mental states are identical, it is hard to see how the course of our lives could be other than the one that is required by the physical determination of the body. What happens to me could, in principle, be known and predicted entirely from adequate knowledge of my body, and the factors in my physical surroundings which impinge upon it.[3]

For these reasons, then, I maintain that mind is ontologically distinct from its bodily conditions. Yet 'mind' itself requires further elucidation. Some philosophers - notably Hume - have attempted to define mind in terms of mental states that are wholly unconnected. On this view there is no self or ego that unites these states and constitutes personal identity. It seems to me clear that we are bound to postulate such a self on at least four grounds. First, unless we postulate it we cannot explain cognition. Only a single and enduring self can relate and unify experiences in the manner that even sense perception requires. In order to know anything - to recognize it as a 'thing' - we need to interrelate and synthesize sense-data; but this activity of interrelating and synthesizing implies a unitary interrelater and synthesizer. Secondly, memory implies that the one who remembers remains the same throughout the past and the present. Thirdly, there is the fact of subjective experience to which I have already referred. To take the same example, a feeling of pain implies a person whose pain it is. To say 'a pain is felt' inevitably invites the question 'by whom?' Lastly, unless there is an identical self persisting throughout its varied experiences moral responsibility could not exist. A person can be held responsible for his past actions only if he is the *same* person in the present as he was in the past.

However, the nature of the self that remains the same throughout its experiences can be misinterpreted in two ways. First, it can be regarded as a pure ego that exists independently of all experiences. Secondly, it can be regarded as an object that can be inspected, described and defined like objects in the physical world. Both forms of misinterpretation occur in Hume's *Treatise.* There he writes that 'I never can catch *myself* at any time without a perception, and never can observe anything but the perception'.[4] Hume presupposes that if there is a unitary and unifying self it must exist in a pure, characterless, state and that it must be accessible to observation. Yet the self is always characterized by a state or activity. Also it is a wholly unique entity that is known only in a subjective manner by an act of self-awareness that is correspondingly unique. Hence a definition of it and of the awareness by which it is known is impossible.

In affirming the soul's distinctness from the body I do not mean to imply any disparagement of the latter. Obviously in this life each person forms a unity in whch the body is as necessary to the mind as the mind is to the body. Moreover the body, like other material things, possesses its own worth. Christians have special reasons for emphasizing these facts. God, they affirm, assumed a human body in Christ; and Christ in turn at the Last Supper consecrated bread and wine as sacramental signs of his approaching sacrifice. Hence the Hebraic stress on man's psychosomatic unity is to be welcomed, and Gnostic dualism is to be avoided.

Nevertheless, spirit transcends matter, and mind transcends body. So far as ordinary human persons are concerned the modes of this transcendence are obvious. They are exemplified in every intelligent word, and in every moral choice. In Christ there is a unique mode corresponding to the uniqueness of the Incarnation. His human nature existed solely through its hypostatic union with the divine nature; and the latter is wholly incorporeal. Also, although the eucharist imparts a new, supernatural, significance to matter it does so only because its spiritual component - the life of the exalted Christ - transcends and informs the material signs.

I come now to my second question. Is belief in the existence of the soul as something distinct from the body required for belief in the continued existence of a person after death? I hold that it is so. Our present, material, bodies will be destroyed at death. Either they will be left to gradual disintegration (for example, in a grave) or they will be immediately dissolved (for example, in a crematorium). These facts are empirically incontestable. Also they impart to death its final meaning and terror. If, then, a human person is to survive, his survival must depend on the continuance of a non-material entity.

However, there is one other possibility I must consider. It may be maintained that even if our mental processes are merely functions of our bodies we can still entertain the hope of immortality on the assumption that in the next life we shall acquire new bodies that will constitute us as persons then, as our present bodies constitute us as persons now. This view seems to me to be untenable for the following reasons.

(i) A new body would not in itself be sufficient to constitute a person as the same self. Let us take an example from art. A painting may be faithfully imitated; but the imitation would not be the same as the original. The imitation would not be the same even if the original were destroyed. Similarly even if a body exactly like mine in terms of mental functions were to be created in another world it would not be the same self that once lived on earth. 'I' should not survive. Someone exactly like me would take my place.

(ii) If my survival were to consist solely in the mental functions of a new body I should be in a constant state of self-deception. A condition of self-identity is that a person is capable of remembering himself as being the same person at t3 as he was at t1 and t2. Yet even if my new body were to be provided with memories of what I took to be my former self they would be deceitful; for I should not be the same self but only a replica of my former one. I should be constantly deceiving myself into remembering myself as the same although in fact I should be someone wholly new.

(iii) What kind of body will my new one be? If my mind consists solely in functions of the material body I now possess my new body must also be a material one. Yet a material body is by nature mortal, and so the expectation of my new body could not constitute the hope of immortality. If I were to survive indefinitely I should need an endless succession of bodies. Where, then, will these bodies exist? Will it be in this world or in another world? The problems involved in any answer we give to these questions are insuperable. In any case such new bodies could come into existence only through the creative act of an omnipotent God. But the view that God would continually re-create us as mortal beings is contrary to the whole Christian concept of him.[5]

The third question is whether the existence of a disembodied soul is conceivable. Some thinkers have maintained that it is inconceivable on the ground that even if the soul is ontologically distinct from the body its operations are dependent on the body so that it cannot survive the extinction of the body. This conclusion is unnecessary. Gecause A is dependent on B in one phase of its existence it need not be so in all phases of it. Thus a child is wholly dependent on its mother in its pre-natal life; but it becomes progressively independent of her until the independence is complete. Even in this life the mind transcends the body by governing it according to its own intentions and values. Moreover, there is no reason why a disembodied soul should not exist eternally. In our present embodied state our mental powers often decay through physical causes; but they need not decay when these causes are removed.

Three further objections to the idea of disembodied existence are that the body is necessary in order to individuate persons, to make them recognizable to each other, and to enable them to communicate with each other. I hold that these objections are answerable. First, the body is not the only principle of individuation. Each human mind is individuated non-corporeally, first by its subject-self or ego, and secondly by the characteristics it acquires in the course of its history. Admittedly these characteristics are mediated through the body and its spatial location; but in themselves they are non-bodily and non-spatial. Each person is aware of his individuated *psyche* and of at least some among its properties in all his mental acts.

The problem of recognition is more difficult, but it is not insoluble. Of course in this life each person is recognized by other persons through his bodily operations. Yet he is recognized in his mental as well as his corporeal individuality. And since this is so I do not see why we should not be capable of recognizing each other as pure spirits in another world. And if we shall be capable of recognizing each other non-corporeally we shall be capable also of thus communicating with each other. Even in this life there are pointers to non-corporeal recognition and communication. Thus I can recognize my friend through the slenderest of physical media (for example by the inflection of his voice). Also through the power of memory I can bring to mind his whole character and even form visual images of him. It is not inconceivable that this power should be so increased that I could discern my friend's actual presence incorporeally. So far as non-bodily communication is concerned the nearest analogy is telepathy. Even if the existence of the latter is not regarded as having been empirically proved there remains the fact of the wordless communion that can exist between two persons. This can reach the point where the two know what is in each other's mind so that they can act on the assumption of this unspoken knowledge.

The question of recognition can be re-expressed through the question of the criteria for ascribing identity to another person. Three criteria are normally proposed: bodily continuity, memory and persistent character-traits. We feel confident that a person is the same at t4 as he was at t1 if (a) he has the same bodily appearance, (b) he remembers events in his past history, and (c) he possesses the same qualities of character. It has been claimed that (b) and (c) are insufficient without (a). It seems to me that in terms of this life the claim is correct. However, because corporeal continuity of a material kind is a necessery condition of ascribing identity to a person in this life it need not be a necessary condition of ascribing identity in another life. There are no *a priori* or empirical grounds for precluding the possibility that in the next life we shall know other souls by an intuitive awareness that will remove the need for any 'criteria' for establishing their identities.

These considerations must be put in a religious context. In reflecting on a future life that is incorporeal we must take account of the fact that according to Christian theism God will confer new powers on the soul in the life to come. The sheer capacity for being free from the ravages of physical mortality is such a power. Christians cannot at any point rightly conceive the next life solely by an extension of the knowledge that we have of ourselves in this life. All I am claiming is that this knowledge does not prevent us from believing, but on the contrary encourages us to believe, that by a new act of creative energy God could grant us an incorporeal mode of existence. We cannot imagine this mode simply because the next life is, in all its aspects, unimaginable.

Another objection to the idea of disembodied existence is that it would be a shadowy, emaciated, kind of sub-existence that would produce dreariness rather than joy. Obviously many of our present joys are physically caused. Yet the view that life would be dull and pointless without them is contrary to two axioms of theism. First, material joys have value only in so far as they have spiritual significance. Secondly, man's 'end' is the vision of God in his incorporeal being. Furthermore, in the life to come we shall continue to have memories of our present, corporeal, state. And these will be transfigured by a spiritual glory that we cannot possess on earth.

However, even if an incorporeal life is possible the question remains whether our future existence will have a bodily character. This question gains its force from the fact that Christians profess belief in the resurrection of the body. I shall assume that this belief cannot be taken with the literalism that has often accompanied it in the past. The view that our present, material, bodies will be re-assembled from the particles that compose them is grotesque. In any case such resurrected bodies would be mortal. If we are to have immortal bodies in the next life they must be new ones that, though exhibiting continuity with our present bodies, will be perfect vehicles for our souls. For want of a better word we can follow Paul's usage in 1 Corinthians 15 and call such bodies 'spiritual'.

Obviously we cannot form any conception of a spiritual body. We can only affirm, with H. H. Price, that it will be 'intermediate between the physical and the mental as we ordinarily conceive of them'.[6] Yet we also cannot form a conception of disembodied existence. Moreover, Christ's resurrection-appearances indicate the possibility of a bodily existence that is other than our present material one. However, it seems to me that the grounds for believing that we shall have spiritual bodies are indecisive. I have already rejected two of them - that a disembodied existence is impossible, and that even if it were possible it would be joyless. It must further be noted that any joys inherent in a spiritual body would be constituted, not by a continuation of the joys inherent in our present bodies, but by the soul of which the spiritual body would be a perfect instrument. The chief theological ground for holding that the future life will be a bodily one is the resurrection of Christ. Yet we cannot infer from his resurrection that we shall have resurrection-bodies. In general we cannot assume that Christ's humanity was exactly like ours. On the contrary if he was God incarnate he must have been unlike, as well as like, other men. In particular there is no exact resemblance between Christ's resurrection-body and any new bodies we might possess. Christ's tomb was found empty; but our bodies will decay or be annihilated. Again, Christ appeared in a new form within this present world of space and time; but no deceased Christian thus appears. In any case the hope of immortality refers to another world.

I do not wish to deny that we shall have spiritual bodies or that they could discharge functions analogous to the functions discharged by our present bodies of flesh. Yet for the reasons I have given I am agnostic on the point. Of course Christians who share my agnosticism must come to terms with the creeds. The Apostles' creed expresses belief in the resurrection of the body while the Nicene creed refers more generally to the 'resurrection of the dead'. Yet even if we believe that our future life may be a disembodied one we can still give these phrases meaning. We can take them to mean that our future life will fulfil our bodily life on earth; that it will be due, not to any power of immortality that we inherently possess, but to a creative act of God; and that it will take the form of participation in the eternal life won for us by Christ as our risen Lord.

What, then are the grounds for belief in immortality? There are no purely rational grounds for it. The most obvious ground is that the soul is by its nature immortal. But this ground is contrary both to the facts of experience and to the primary convictions of theism. It is contrary to the facts of experience in so far as although the soul is ontologically distinct from the body it still now needs the body as the basis of its operation; so that although it is capable of surviving the body it does not possess any intrinsic power of survival. The belief that the soul is by nature immortal is also contrary to theism; for anything exists only so

long as God wills it to exist; and whether he will endow the soul with a
new form of existence after its separation from the body is for him
alone to decide. In other words does belief in him entail belief in
immortality?

There are two general reasons for affirming this entailment. The first
is that because God is infinitely just he must desire the rectification of
his creatures' unmerited sufferings and the fulfilment of those spiritual
potentialities that have been undeservedly frustrated on earth.
Although this argument is convincing it is insufficient. It is
inapplicable to those who have not suffered undeservedly to a morally
questionable degree. It is also inapplicable to those who have
actualized their potentialities, if not completely, at least to an extent
that leaves no reasonable grounds for complaint. Furthermore it does
not prove that the future life will be endless. For a proof of this we must
turn to another argument that I stated at the end of chapter one.
Because God is pure love he must desire the highest good for persons
whom he made in his image. This good is that they should enjoy
communion with him, not merely in a clouded fashion for a few years,
but 'face to face' eternally. Certainly eternal life is a further gift that
God bestows on us. Yet the gift proceeds from the same love that
moved him to create us in the first place. Even on the human plane a
person does not deliberately withdraw his presence from a person
whom he loves. Still less will God deliberately terminate his relation
with his human creatures whom he loves infinitely. This argument
becomes even clearer when we consider God's love in the order of
redemption. If God so loved us that he became man for us it is
inconceivable that he should desire anything less for us than eternal life
with him.

Yet the ground that most Christians would give for their hope of
immortality is Christ's resurrection. According to the New Testament
the Resurrrection signifies two thing. First, Christ's tomb was found
empty. Secondly he re-appeared to his disciples for a brief period in a
body that was both like and unlike the body that had been crucified.
We cannot describe the structure of Christ's resurrection-body
because the latter was, and always will remain, without any kind of
analogy in our own existence. For the same reason we cannot describe
the mode of transition from Christ's old body to his new one. The only
question we can validly ask (which in any case is the only question that
concerns me now) is whether the Resurrection proves our immortality.
If taken solely in itself it does not prove it. It might have signified no
more than a temporary revival of Christ's life in a new form. Even if it
had necessarily signified that Christ's new life was an eternal one it
would not have necessarily also signified that eternal life will be
obtained by his disciples. The Resurrection constitutes a ground for
belief in immortality only when it is seen in the light of the Incarnation,
the Exaltation and the gift of the Spirit.

The basic fact is the Incarnation. If Jesus was God incarnate he must
have been immortal. The hypostatic union entails Christ's immortality

in two ways. First, his person was divine and so eternal. He was constituted as an individual by the co-existence of his human nature with the divine nature in the person of the Word. Because of this we can, according to what is known as the *communicatio idiomatum,* attribute to Christ's human nature properties belonging to his divine nature; and we can attribute to his divine nature properties belonging to his human nature. It is the first mode of attribution that concerns me now. Because the human Christ was personalized by the eternal Son we can ascribe to him the eternity that characterizes God alone, and we can worship him accordingly. Secondly, Christ's divine nature constantly activated his human nature with an immediacy and a completeness that can have no parallel in any other man. His human life was a finite embodiment of God's own eternal life, a veiled presence of God's indestructible glory, a living image of the endless communion that the Son enjoys with the Father in the unity of the Holy Spirit. Hence the human Jesus is, by a necessity of his own nature in its ontological relation to the divine nature, the same yesterday, today and for ever'.[7] The sameness is presupposed by the whole Christian experience of him as one who mediates the very life and love of God himself.

Christ's resurrection, therefore, while being a new phase in the life of his humanity, was an inevitable consequence of the Incarnation. It was a further revelation in the spatio-temporal sphere of the eternal life he already possessed by virtue of his union with the Godhead. His person as the incarnate Son was both the ground of his resurrection and the reason why his resurrection can be taken to signify the entrance of eternal life into the present world of space and time. This does not mean that the Resurrection was a dispensable episode in his embodiment of God's eternal life. On the contrary it was this embodiment's culmination. It was necessary for him to die in order to live a fully human life. And the mode of his death was inevitable if he was to obey the divine will in the conditions of his time and place. The Resurrection proved his victory over both death and the sin by which his death was caused.

Next there is the Exaltation. Christ (as the New Testament puts it) was exalted to the right hand of God. This of course is symbolical language. If pressed literally it would or could be seriously misleading in two ways. It would imply that heaven is a physical place above the earth. Also, it could imply that after death Christ achieved a closer union with God than the one he had previously possessed, and that he acquired an eternal form of life that he previously lacked. Yet there can be no closer union with God than the hypostatic union that Jesus possessed from the first moment of his conception. And through this union he always had an eternal form of being. The language of exaltation means that he now shares God's eternal life, not in a veiled state of humiliation, but in an unveiled state of glory. The Resurrection appearances were temporary expressions of this glory in a spatial mode. The glory itself is concealed from human sight.

Finally the exalted Christ sent and sends the Holy Spirit in order to communicate his eternal life to believers. Here it is necessary to recollect the ontological nature of the supernatural transformation wrought in the soul by the Spirit. Whoever is united to Christ is a 'new creature'. The first form of life we receive from God through the order of creation is by nature mortal even if God, out of his infinite generosity, chooses to grant us immortality. However, the second form of life that Christians receive from Christ is by nature eternal. While remaining creatures who are wholly distinct from God they receive the inherently eternal life of Christ's divinized humanity. I say that Christians 'receive', not 'will receive', Christ's life. They receive it even now in a partial and veiled way; but they will receive it fully only after they have passed through death, and entered another world in which there will be no evil or impediment of any kind to our love for God and for each other. Therefore the presence of both 'realized' and 'futurist' elements in New Testament eschatology is inevitable.

This eternal life cannot be assessed in merely quantitative terms. Its nature does not consist merely in the fact that it is endless; for it is possible to conceive a life of damnation that has no end. The everlasting life embodied in and conveyed by Christ is distinctively constituted by its quality which has two dominant aspects: obedience and love. The human Jesus's reception of the eternal life granted to him through the hypostatic union was proved by his perfect obedience to the Father and his perfect love for his Father's creatures. Therefore Christians can receive the eternal life of Christ only to the extent that they imitate his obedience and love. So far as love is concerned the heart of the matter was expressed thus by the author of 1 John: 'We know that we have passed out of death into life because we love the breathren'.[8]

This, then, is the basis of Christain belief in immortality. In the next section I shall deal with questions relating to the destiny that awaits each person after death.[9]

According to a Christian belief that has its origins in Judaism each person will encounter divine judgment after death. This judgment has often been conceived in anthropomorphic terms that do not represent it adequately. Its nature will be simple. It will consist in God's verdict concerning, first, each person's spiritual state and, secondly, the effects that the state entails. Obviously we cannot imagine the form that the verdict will take. The only question open to us is this. What will be the possible consequences of God's judgment for this or that person? Christians have believed that there will be three possible consequences: Heaven, Purgatory and Hell. Within the Western Church both Roman Catholics and Protestants have usually believed in the first and third of these although only Catholics have usually believed in the second. The first and second are not mutually exclusive. It can be held that even if some souls will go immediately to Heaven, others will go there only after passing through Purgatory. I shall now examine the meaning that can be attached to these concepts.

The concept of Heaven is the easiest to elucidate although it is one to which we cannot give content in terms of our present experience. Heaven will consist primarily in the vision of God and in the perfect knowledge of other persons in the light of him. It will also consist in the perfect knowledge of the ways in which God has been redemptively present in our terrestrial lives. Finally it will consist in the transfiguration of our terrestrial experiences by the divine glory revealed in Christ. We cannot specify this final beatitude in further detail. And so I agree with these words written by A. E. Taylor towards the end of his life. 'It is wisest and safest to commit ourselves only to one definite assertion, that to be in Heaven, as Christianity conceives of it, is to be a member of a society of persons who see God, themselves, and each other as all truly are, without confusion or illusion, and who love God, themselves and each other with the love of this true insight; what is more than this is imaginative mythology.'[10]

The theological difficulties are caused by the ideas of Purgatory and Hell. Before discussing them it is necessary to clarify the concept of a punishment or penalty inflicted on sinners. I touched on this in my chapter on the Atonement, and I shall now have occasion to restate some of the views I expressed there. How, then, does sin incur a penalty? It can do so in two ways of which the first is intrinsic and the second extrinsic. The intrinsic penalty is the corruption of soul and alienation from God that sin entails. An extrinsic penalty would be an additional punishment that God inflicts on the sinner either in this life or in the life to come. All sinners bear the first penalty. This is inevitable. It exemplifies a law of cause and effect that is as inexorable in the spiritual world as similar laws are in the physical world. Christ did not pay this penalty in our stead; for it is one that only the sinner himself can pay. Rather Christ, by his unmerited grace, delivers us from the penalty by freeing us from sin's guilt and power.

However, will God inflict an extrinsic penalty or additional punishment in the life to come? Many Christians have affirmed that he will do so; and the fear of such a punishment has often dominated their lives. In dealing with the question it is necessary to distinguish between legal and theological concepts of punishment. Because extrinsic forms of punishment are (rightly) imposed by legal systems it does not follow that they must be imposed by God. My own view is that they are not imposed by God, and that sin's intrinsic penalty is theologically sufficient. We must futher distinguish between penitent and impenitent sinners. Penitent sinners need have no fear of punishment; for their sins have already been forgiven by God. In a personal relationship forgiveness and a demand for the punishment of the one forgiven are mutually exclusive.

Yet will not God inflict an extra punishment on the impenitent? I do not think so, for two reasons. First, there can be no greater penalty than separation from God and from the society of those who love him.

Also there can be no spiritual pain that exceeds the pain that this alienation entails. Hence those who try to envisage an extra punishment for unrepentant sinners are bound to describe it in terms of physical torment. Yet these terms are inapplicable to a non-material mode of being. Secondly, extra punishment would not serve any good. Even in this life (so I maintain) punishment cannot be justified solely on the grounds of retribution. It must also be shown to be deterrent (that is, to deter either the offender or others from committing a similar offence). Now, in a future life extrinsic punishment cannot deter the sinner because there are no further sins that he can commit. Yet could not the thought of such future punishment deter others from committing sin in this present life? Undoubtedly it could do so and has done so. Nevertheless, the intrinsic penalty of sin is sufficient to deter those who realize its horrifying character.

The distinction between intrinsic and extrinsic forms of punishment is paralleled by the distinction between intrinsic and extrinsic forms of reward. There will be one reward for the good and the penitent, and another for the evil and the impenitent. Yet just as we must not envisage the first reward as something additional to the vision of God, so we must not envisage the second as something additional to separation from him. And just as the only valid motive for desiring the first reward is the love of God himself, so the only valid motive for dreading the second is the fear of separation from him.

In the light of these reflections on sin's penalty I shall consider the meanings that, in my view, ought to be attached to Purgatory and Hell. Because I regard forgiveness and punishment as being mutually exclusive I cannot conceive of Purgatory as a sphere in which Christians painfully discharge a penalty that is still due to sins that have been forgiven. However, the idea of Purgatory is, I believe, convincing if it is regarded as a purificatory process whereby souls are gradually cleansed of sin and so made fit for eternal communion with God. The ground for postulating Purgatory as a process of spiritual purification is this. Most people (including Christians) at death are far from being fit for the vision of God. They remain subject to sinful impulses, and often reject God in their acts even if they confess him in their words. If, then, they are to enjoy the vision of God immediately they can do so only if he transforms them, by a sudden act, after their death. Yet such a sudden transformation would be discontinuous with the way in which, during this present life, God gradually transforms us through the consent of our own wills. And so it is reasonable to suppose that after this life God will continue his transformation of us in a like manner. The difference will be that whereas in this life we are free to give or to withhold our consent to God's will, in Purgatory we shall give our consent spontaneously in the certain hope of the bliss to which our purification leads. I say that it is 'reasonable' to suppose this. Yet in such a speculative matter human reasoning does not necessarily correspond to divine intention. We cannot *know* in advance the means by which God intends to bring sinful, but faithful,

Christians into eternal fellowship with himself.

So far as Hell is concerned I have already stated my opinion. The idea of an 'extra' punishment for unrepentant sinners is invalid. If there is a Hell it will consist wholly in the soul's final separation from God. This separation is bound to cause inconceivable pain. The condemned sinner would be consumed by a frustration and a despair that fully justify everything that has been imaginatively written concerning the tortures of the damned. Would such pain be everlasting? The idea that it would be so seems scarcely compatible with either God's justice or his love. It is, I think, better to assume that such souls would be ultimately annihilated. Because they are spiritually dead, complete death would be their fitting end. Yet this view also is speculative. Again, we cannot *know*. In any case some theologians (notably Origen) have held that all men will ultimately be saved. I shall discuss this opinion in answering the second of two questions that now arise.

First, shall we be given a 'second chance' after death to accept or to reject God? The traditional answer to this question is a negative one. It has been commonly taught that each person's destiny will be sealed at the moment of his death. However, there are four grounds for affirming that for all persons there will be the possibility of a fresh choice after death for or against God. First, to many people God does not present himself in this life as an object of choice. Many have either no concept of the Divine or a false one. Many too do not posses a full knowledge even of moral goodness. Heredity or environment has radically weakened their moral perception and their capacity for moral choice. Secondly death, and sometimes the process of dying, will put the whole of our lives in a final perspective and so enable us to make a final choice. Thirdly, even for Christians God and his providential ways are largely hidden in this life. We do not yet see him 'face to face' and so cannot yet make an epistemologically clear choice for or against him. Lastly, even Christians remain sinners who never make an absolute choice between good and evil. All except the saints constantly hover between the love of God that brings eternal life and the love of themselves that brings eternal death.

An objection to the possibility of a fresh choice after death is that it would make this life spiritually pointless or at least rob it of the spiritual importance that theists have usually ascribed to it. I do not think that this objection can be sustained. If there will be a new and final choice beyond death it will be integrally related to the choices we have made on earth. In so far as we have freely chosen good we shall be disposed to a final choice that will lead us to God; but in so far we have chosen evil we shall be disposed to a final choice that will lead us away from him. Even in this life each good choice strengthens our wills for choosing good in the future. Similarly our wills are weakened by every evil choice. And so a final choice beyond death would complete a pattern that is exhibited within this present world. Yet, in spite of the arguments I have given, the limits of our mortal vision prevent us from affirming with certainty that such a choice will be granted.

The second question concerns universalism. Will all men ultimately be saved or will some be excluded for ever from the presence of God? This is another question that we cannot answer with certainty. The testimony of the New Testament is ambiguous. Also the theological arguments for and against universalism are inconclusive. The two main arguments for it are that because God is pure love he would not have created a world in which some men could be finally lost, and that because every man is made in his image no man can finally resist his love. The two main arguments against universalism are that the free will given to all men by God makes it possible that some men will finally reject him, and that if it were known that all men will ultimately be saved this knowledge would remove the sense of urgency in the Gospel's call to repentance.

As I have said, I do not find any of these arguments conclusive. On the one hand the arguments for universalism based on an appeal to God's love are obviously attractive. Yet against them we must set the facts that human freedom is itself a gift of God's love; that God respects our freedom in all his dealings with us; and that therefore his love does not exclude the possibility that some men may reject him. The closest analogy here is that of a father who, while doing all he can for his erring son, does not force him to mend his ways but patiently hopes for amendment. If the son does not repent the father can do no more although his love does not cease. On the other hand against the argument based on free will it could be said that the love of God infinitely exceeds the love of any human father; that no human son exists by an act of creation *ex nihilo* on the part of his father; and that these differences entail the view that every human creature will finally accept God's love - not by capitulating to an irresistible force, but by freely recognizing in God, when all else has failed, the source of his well-being. There remains the argument that if all men will ultimately be saved, and if this can be foreknown, the urgency in the Gospel's call to repentance is removed. This argument presupposes that the fear of hell is the only motive for repentance. However, although it has often been a motive, the only finally valid motive from a Christian standpoint is love for God in answer to his love for us. I therefore conclude that a proper attitude to universalism is an agnostic one. Because we cannot disprove it and because there is some scriptural support for it we cannot justifiably reject it. Yet because of the scriptural texts and theological arguments that tell against it we can treat it only as an hypothesis that will not be verified or falsified until the life to come.

I am well aware that some of my readers will not share the agnosticism I have expressed concerning the possible forms of human life in the world to come. Yet such agnosticism (that will doubtless be shared by other readers) need not disturb us. After all, even if we are confident in stating the general forms of life beyond death we cannot predict the destiny of any particular person. Even if we are universalists we cannot predict the way or ways in which God will ultimately save all mankind. In any case for the purpose of sustaining hope we need to hold only three beliefs that, in my view, belong to the core of Christian theism. These are that God is infinite and unfailing in both his power and his love; that he forgives all penitent sinners; and that the goal he intends for all his human creatures is that they should receive the eternal life of the exalted Christ. The true Christian is one who consciously receives this life partly and under a veil here and now, in the sure hope of receiving it fully and in an unveiled mode hereafter. And so I shall conclude with words from Aquinas's eucharistic hymn *Adoro te devote, latens Deitas:*

> O Christ, whom now beneath a veil we see
> May what we thirst for soon our portion be
> There in the glory of thy dwelling-place
> To gaze on thee unveiled and see thy face.

[1] *Death and Eternal Life* (london 1976, p 115).

[2] 1 Cor. 13. 3.

[3] *The Self and Immortality* (London 1973, p 64). Lewis has argued at length for the ontological distinctness of mind in his Gifford Lectures entitled *The Elusive Mind* (London 1969).

[4] 1. 4. 6.

[5] In his *Death and Eternal Life* John Hick has suggested that after death we shall receive 'replicas' of our present material bodies. His suggestion has been cogently criticized by Paul Badham (*Christian Beliefs about Life after Death*), London 1976, chap. 4). However, it is only fair to add that Hick admits that 'it is conceivable that in the resurrection world we shall have bodies which are the outward reflection of our inner nature but which reflect it in ways quite different from that in which our present bodies reflect our personality' (op. cit., p 295).

[6] *Essays in the Philosophy of Religion* (Oxford 1972, p 114).

[7] Heb. 13. 8.

[8] 1 Jn. 3. 14.

[9] There are some elements in Christian eschatology with which I am not immediately concerned. But I must mention and briefly state my views on three that are closely interconnected: the belief in the so-called 'Second Coming' of Christ, the concept of the 'end' of the world and the hope of a renewed *cosmos*. I shall assume that we cannot validly take belief in the *parousia* to mean that Christ will re-appear within the confines of this present world which could not contain him in his glorified state. Rather, remembering that *parousia* can signify both 'coming' and 'presence', we should think of Christ's last 'coming' as the final mode in which he is present to men. He was first present in the flesh, and then in his risen power; he is present now through the Holy Spirit; and he will be finally present in an unveiled mode in which he will appear to all men as their Judge and Saviour. So far as the 'end' of the world is concerned it is obvious that the cessation of human life on this planet, or even this planet's extinction, bears no necessary relation to to the Christian hope that refers to another and a better world. What, then, are we to say concerning the idea of a renewed *cosmos?* I have already given my answer with regard to human beings when I suggested that, while it is possible that we shall have spiritual bodies, even an incorporeal life would preserve our present corporeal experiences through a transfigured memory of them. Will, then, the sub-human entities of this planet survive, in a new form, hereafter? Because they lack souls capable of survival I do not see how they could do so. Yet here too we ought to be agnostic. We cannot know God's intention for other terrestrial species (and *a fortiori* not for species that may exist in other worlds). We know only his intention for our own species; for he has supernaturally communicated this intention by becoming one of us. Yet even here we know only in part.

[10] *The Christian Hope of Immortality* (London 1946, pp 69-70).

Appendix
John Hick on Christianity and Other Religions

As I said in my Preface, I shall examine John Hick's views on the above subject and, thereby, also his views on belief in the Incarnation because he crystallizes two of the major questions facing the theologian today: first, what is the relation between Christian theism and the truth-claims made by other religions, and secondly, what are the status and meaning that we today must give to the traditional belief that in Christ God became man for our salvation? I shall take as my source Hick's *God Has Many Names* (London 1980). All my references, unless otherwise stated, will be to this book which sums up views that Hick has been expressing in various writings during recent years.

Hick's basic contention is that we are required to undergo 'a "Copernican revolution" in our theology of religions, consisting in a paradigm shift from a Christianity-centred or Jesus-centred to a God-centred model of the universe of faiths. One then sees the great world religions as different human responses to the one divine Reality, embodying different perceptions which have been formed in different historical and cultural circumstances' (pp 5-6). Hick does not predict or even desire the emergence of a single world religion. 'For the different religious traditions, with their complex internal differentiations, have developed to meet the needs of the range of mentalities expressed in the different human cultures' (p 7). All religions are 'inevitably limited and imperfect, each having its own distinctive strengths and weaknesses, advantages and disadvantages. And in the new ecumenical age which we are now entering the religious traditions will increasingly interact with one another and affect one another's further development, enabling each to learn, we may hope, from the others' insights and benefit from the others' virtues' (p 8). Hick then proceeds to quote from the literature of Islam, the Sikh faith and Bhakti-Hinduism to substantiate his thesis that 'human beings are coming together to open their minds to a higher reality, which is thought of as the personal creator and Lord of the universe, and as making vital moral demands upon the lives of men' (p 45). Hick then amplifies this a little later by affirming 'that there is but one God, who is maker and lord of all; that in his infinite fullness and richness of being he exceeds all our human attempts to grasp him in thought; and that the devout in the various great world religions are in fact worshipping that one God, but through different, overlapping concepts or mental icons of him' (pp 48-9). Hick therefore concludes that 'the older Christian view of other faiths as areas of spiritual darkness within which there is no salvation, no knowledge of God, and no acceptable worship must be mistaken' (p 49). Hence Christian theologians, especially Roman Catholic ones, 'have been making strenuous efforts to escape from the unacceptable implications of the older view, though usually without feeling entitled explicitly to renounce it' (*ibid*).

What, then, does all this imply for belief in the Incarnation? Here Hick largely repeats what he said in his contribution to *The Myth of God Incarnate*. The belief is not a statement of objective fact; it is 'a poetic, or symbolic, or mythological statement'. 'It is a way of saying that Jesus is our living contact with the transcendent God. In his presence we find that we are brought into the presence of God. We believe that he is so truly God's servant that in living as his disciples we are living according to the divine purpose. And as our sufficient and saving point of contact with God there is something absolute about him which justifies the absolute language which Christianity has developed' (p 55). Hick expands this view of Jesus as follows on p 65: 'Thus in Jesus' presence we should have felt that we are in the presence of God - not in the sense that the man Jesus literally *is* God, but in the sense that he was so totally conscious of God that we could catch something of that consciousness by spiritual contagion.' On p 72 Hick recurs to the term 'myth' for an explanation of incarnational language. 'A myth', he writes, 'is a story which is told but which is not literally true, or an idea or image which is applied to someone or something but which does not literally apply, but which invites a particular attitude in its hearers. Thus the truth of a myth is a kind of practical truth consisting in the appropriatenenss of the attitude to its object.' The myth 'expresses a disciple's commitment to Jesus as his personal Lord' (*ibid.*) Hick even goes so far as to call the myth 'the hyperbole of the heart' (p 78). He further contends that belief in an objective incarnation was conditioned by the religious culture in which Christianity arose. 'It is clear that ideas of divinity embodied in human life were widespread in the ancient world, so that there is nothing surprising in the deification of Jesus in that cultural environment' (p 67). A different environment would have produced a different interpretation of Jesus. 'If the Christian gospel had moved east, into India, instead of West, into the Roman empire, Jesus' religious significance would probably have been expressed by hailing him within Hindu culture as a divine Avatar, and within the Mahayana Buddhism which was then developing in India as a Bodhisattva, one who has attained to oneness with Ultimate Reality but remains in the human world out of compassion for mankind and to show others the way of life' (pp 69-70). Therefore 'the doctrines of Incarnation and Trinity may turn out to be part of the "intellectual" construction which has to be left behind when the disciple of Jesus discards the cultural packaging in which western Christianity has wrapped the gospel' (p 87). Hick offers two further criticisms of belief in an objective incarnation of God in Christ. First, to affirm that the human Jesus was also God 'is as paradoxical as to say that this circle drawn with a pencil on paper is also a square' (p 71). Secondly, the affirmation implies the exclusive claim that non-Christians are outside the sphere of salvation (p 73).

I wish immediately to express agreement with Hick on two fundamental points that I have already made in this book. First, non-Christian theists have a knowledge of God. Secondly this knowledge can minister to their salvation. The difference between Christians and non-Christians is that through the Incarnation Christians obtain a supernatural mode of knowledge culminating in a supernatural mode of salvation in which all natural modes are, or will be, fulfilled. I should further admit that some saving knowledge of God is obtainable by those who adhere to non-theistic forms of religion in so far as (a) they apprehend a spiritual reality infinitely transcending this finite world of space and time, (b) they make the knowledge of this reality the chief aim of life and (c) they find in this knowledge a way of redemption in terms of those spiritual and moral values that a theist can endorse. In this whole area there is an endless complexity that only God can wholly unravel. Thus a non-theistic Hindu or Buddhist could be nearer to God than a merely 'nominal' theist or a theist whose view of God is radically anthropomorphic or self-centred. In short I gladly admit the widest possible scope to Jacques Maritain's judgment that 'under many names, names which are not that of God, in ways known only to God, the interior act of a soul's thought can be directed towards a reality which in fact truly may be God'. (I take this quotation from John Baillie's *The Sense of the Presence of God,* London 1962, p 194.)

However, Hick's viewpoint compels me to raise the following queries that all go to the heart of the matter.

1. In his attempt to find a common core in the world religions Hick is inevitably selective. He quotes from non-Christian texts which support belief in God as a personal and loving Creator. But he could have quoted an equal amount of evidence that is contrary to this belief. Thus Hinduism also includes an extreme form of monism of which Hick writes as follows. 'The Hinduism which is best known from western textbooks is the advaita-vedanta philosophy according to which the one ultimate reality, beyond the grasp of all human categories including personality, is the Absolute, called Brahman. According to this teaching, all human souls are in the deepest depth of their being one, and the one Atman which they are is in turn ultimately identical with the eternal Brahman" (p 33). Again there is Buddhism in its original non-theistic form. Moreover, in order to make our account of religion complete we must reckon with all the manifestations of polytheism and animism.

2. We cannot evade the conflict between religious beliefs and the question of objective truth that the conflict raises. On p 5 Hick says that it is inappropriate to ask 'Which is the true religion?' Admittedly I should not wish to put the question in such general terms. Nevertheless, so far as the transcendental truth claims of religion are concerned the question of objective truth remains. Thus divine reality cannot be both personal and impersonal. Also it cannot be validly interpreted both in theistic and in monistic terms. To look at it from the human side, our final bliss cannot consist both in the attainment of

Nirvana and in eternal fellowship with a personal God of love. Certainly God infinitely exceeds our understanding. Nevertheless it is one thing to say that he exceeds it as the Creator of the world *ex nihilo;* but it is another thing to say that he exceeds it as a non-personal Absolute with which every soul is, or can become, identical. This brings me to my next query.

3. There are traces of 'cultural relativism' in Hick's description of the differences between various religions. He seems to imply that these differences can be explained by reference to differences in the historical circumstances in which these various religions arose. Thus (in addition to the passages I have already quoted) he writes thus on p 53 of the appearance of different religions in so-called axial period. 'In each case the revelatory experiences, and the religious traditions to which they gave rise, were conditioned by the history, culture, language, climate, and indeed all the concrete circumstances of human life at that particular time and place. Thus the cultural and philosophical form of the revelation of the divine is characteristically different in each case, although we may believe that everywhere the one Spirit has been at work, pressing in upon the human spirit.' However, there are two reasons for rejecting the view (that Hick could be taken to imply) that the factors he mentioned are the *sole* cause of religious differences. First, different forms of religion have arisen in the same circumstances. Secondly, and chiefly, if differences in religious belief were caused solely by secular factors, we should not have any reason for preferring one type of belief to another (e.g. theism to polytheism). I shall consider this question of cultural relativism in more detail with reference to Hick's views on the doctrine of the Incarnation.

4. As Hick recognizes, the crucial question in any assessment of the relation between Christianity and non-Christian religions concerns the status and meaning of the belief in Jesus as God incarnate; for (so I have maintained) it is this belief (with the associated belief in the Trinity) that constitutes Christianity as a supernatural revelation and differentiates it from all other religions. Here I find Hick's view unsatisfactory on three grounds. First, I fail to see what function incarnational language can validly discharge if it does not signify the objective fact that God actually became man in Christ. If (as Hick affirms in language reminiscent of Schleiermacher's christology) Jesus was merely a man who saves us by awakening in us an echo of his own 'God-consciousness' what purpose is served by speaking of him 'mythologically' as God incarnate? Hick tells us that the purpose is to express the truth that 'there is something absolute about Jesus' and to invite an appropriate attitude to its object (namely the attitude of commitment to Jesus as one's Lord). But what is the 'something absolute' if it is not the absoluteness of God himself? And how could an appropriate response to the myth fail to evoke an attitude of complete devotion that is due to God alone? In other words, unless the 'myth' is objectively true the distinctive attitudes it engenders are unwarranted. Hick's description of it as 'the hyperbole of the heart'

suggests that it merely expresses an emotional attitude inherited from an intellectually discredited tradition. If so the sooner it is discarded the better. Furthermore, Hick's attempt to explain the origins of belief in the Incarnation by reference to its cultural environment is untenable; for it is clear (as Dunn has most recently shown) that there is nothing in the religious background to primitive Christianity that could explain the belief's emergence. Hick's suggestion that if Christianity had moved East instead of West Christ would have been interpreted as a divine Avatar or Buddha figure is invalidated by the fact that such an interpretation would have distorted the original Christian belief, reached against a largely Jewish background, that Christ was the absolutely unique incarnation of the personal Creator who is qualitatively different from all his creatures. And Hick himself holds that belief in a personal Creator is the unifying goal of religions today. There are two answers to Hick's further suggestion that the doctrines of the Incarnation and the Trinity are dispensable constructions due to 'the cultural packaging in which western Christianity has wrapped the Gospel'. First, these doctrines were grounded in the first Christians' response to Christ. Secondly, in developing the doctrines through conciliar pronouncements all that the Fathers did was to explicate this response in terms that were as precise as possible but that did not imply adherence to any one system of speculative philosophy.[1] There remain two more criticisms that Hick brings against the doctrine of the Incarnation: that it is paradoxical, and that it implies that non-Christians are outside the sphere of salvation. I have already answered the first question by maintaining that while the doctrine is paradoxical it is not self-contradictory. In answer to the second criticism it is enough to repeat that here, as elsewhere, we must set belief in the Incarnation in the context of belief in God as the Creator. The Word who became man in Christ is the same Word by whom all things were made and who seeks the good of all men through the kindling of the divine image that he has placed upon them.

[1] The expression 'cultural relativism' (or 'relativity') can have two meanings in a religious context. It can mean that religious beliefs are partly or wholly conditioned by their cultural setting. It can also mean that because of this conditioning beliefs that originated in one culture are unintelligible or at least alien to people who belong to another (especially to one far separated in space or time). I am here concerned solely with the first meaning. And my central contention (which is purely a matter of objective scholarship) is that the origins of belief in the Incarnation cannot be explained in terms of its Jewish and Hellenistic background. On the second meaning I would only observe, first that the christological passages in the N.T. I have mentioned seem to me to be sufficiently intelligible in the sense originally given to them; and, secondly, that when taken in this sense they support, by an unbroken process of doctrinal development, the formulations of Nicaea and Chalcedon. (On the second meaning of 'cultural relativism' as a whole in relation to the modern understanding of the N.T. see A. M. Ramsey's acute criticisms of D.E. Nineham in the second chapter of his *Jesus and the Living Past,* Oxford 1980).

INDEX